THE RESILIENT LEADER

LEVERAGE ADVERSITY *to* ADVANCE YOUR TEAM

HarperCollins Leadership

An Imprint of HarperCollins

The Resilient Leader

Published by HarperCollins Leadership, an imprint of HarperCollins Focus LLC.

Published in association with Yates & Yates, www.yates2.com.

ISBN 978-1-4003-5107-7 (ePub)
ISBN 978-1-4003-5106-0 (HC)

Library of Congress Cataloging-in-Publication Data on File

978-1-4003-5106-0

HarperCollins Publishers, Macken House, 39/40 Mayor Street Upper, Dublin 1, D01 C9W8, Ireland (https://www.harpercollins.com).

Printed in the United States of America

26 27 28 29 30 LBC 5 4 3 2 1

Thank you to Charlie Wetzel for his help preparing this book.

CONTENTS

CHAPTER 1

REFRAME YOUR ATTITUDE TOWARD ADVERSITY

In early 2023 software giant SAS completed a survey on resiliency that involved more than 2,400 senior executives working in twelve countries across four continents. Here's what they found:

97 percent viewed resilience as important to business success.

87 percent said resilience helps them prepare for unforeseen events.

53 percent viewed their organizations as lacking resiliency.
46 percent said they are not fully equipped to face disruption.[1]

In essence, they saw a gap between the amount of resilience their organizations needed to be successful and the amount they possessed.

How can organizations close this gap? It starts with the leaders of organizations. Everything rises and falls on leadership. When the leaders of an organization improve, so do the organizations. When the leaders become more resilient, so do the teams and individuals they lead. If your team or organization isn't as resilient as it needs to be or would benefit from becoming more resilient, then *you* need to become more resilient.

CHANGING HOW YOU SEE ADVERSITY

Your growth process in the area of resilience starts with changing your perspective. If you can reframe how you see adversity, it will help you to develop resilience, persevere, lead your team more effectively, and ultimately achieve your goals. So how should you reframe adversity?

1. ACKNOWLEDGE THAT ADVERSITY IS UNAVOIDABLE

Everybody fails, errs, and makes mistakes. You've heard the saying "To err is human, to forgive, divine." Alexander Pope wrote that over three hundred years ago. And he was only paraphrasing a saying that was common two thousand years ago during the time of the Romans. Things today are the same as they were then: If you're a human being, adversity is normal. You're going to make mistakes. You're going to face setbacks. You will need to handle problems, messes, predicaments, and bad luck. And if you're a leader, you'll face more of them than the average person.

You're probably familiar with Murphy's law and the Peter Principle. Recently I came across something called "Rules for Being Human." I think it describes well the state we're in as people:

Rule 1: You will learn lessons.

Rule 2: There are no mistakes—only lessons.

Rule 3: A lesson is repeated until it is learned.

Rule 4: If you don't learn the easy lessons, they get *harder.* (Pain is one way the universe gets your attention.)

Rule 5: You'll know you've learned a lesson when your actions change.[2]

To reframe your attitude toward adversity, embrace the words of writer Norman Cousins, who said, "The essence of man is imperfection." You make mistakes, so accept that.

2. REALIZE THAT FAILURE RARELY COMES AS A SINGLE, ISOLATED EVENT

Growing up, I thought that success and failure came in a moment. The best example I can think of is taking a test. If you got an A, it meant you succeeded; if you got an F, it meant you failed. But I've come to realize that failure is a process. If you flunk a test, it doesn't mean you just failed a one-time event. The F shows that you neglected the process leading up to the test.

In 1997 I wrote a book called *Your Road Map to Success.* It offers a kind of overview on what it means to be successful. In it I define *success* as:

- Knowing your purpose in life
- Growing to reach your potential
- Sowing seeds that benefit others

The thesis of the book is that success is not a destination—a place where you arrive one day. Instead, it is the journey you take. And whether you succeed comes from what you do day to day. In other words, success is a process.

Failure works the same way. It's not someplace you arrive. Just as success is not an event, neither is failure. It's how you deal with life along the way. Resilient people face adversity, bounce back, and become better for what they experienced. And they know that no one can conclude that they've failed until they breathe their last breath. Until then, they're still in process and the jury is still out.

3. RECOGNIZE THAT SUCCESS AND FAILURE ARE SUBJECTIVE

When you err—whether you miscalculate crucial figures, miss a deadline, blow a deal, make a poor choice concerning your children, or otherwise fumble a ball—what determines whether that action was a failure? How do you judge it? Is it determined by the size of the problem it caused or the amount of money it cost you or your organization? Or by how much heat you have to take from your boss or criticism by your peers? Do you let others call what you do failure? Or call *you* a failure?

What are your standards? How do you evaluate any action that falls short of a goal? If an action isn't morally wrong or illegal, is it really a *failure*? You have the right to judge your performance and label what you do because it's subjective. Your *perception* of your actions and your *response* will determine whether your actions were a failure.

RESILIENT PEOPLE FACE ADVERSITY, BOUNCE BACK, AND BECOME BETTER FOR WHAT THEY EXPERIENCED.

Did you know that entrepreneurs almost never get their first business off the ground? Or their second? Or their third? According to former Tulane University business professor Lisa Amoss, the average for entrepreneurs is 3.8 failures before they finally make it in business.[3] They are not deterred by problems, mistakes, or errors. Why? Because they don't see setbacks as failure. They recognize that three steps forward and two steps back *still* equals one step forward. And as a result, they overcome average, become achievers, and develop resilience along the way.

4. DECLARE ADVERSITY NOT TO BE YOUR ENEMY

Most people try to avoid adversity like the plague. They're afraid of it. But it takes adversity to create success. College basketball coach Rick Pitino stated it even more strongly: "Failure is good," he said. "It's fertilizer. Everything I've learned about coaching I've learned from making mistakes."

People who see adversity as the enemy are captive to those who conquer it. Herbert V. Prochnow believed that "the fellow who never makes a mistake takes his orders from one who does." Observe any high achievers, and you'll discover people who don't see a mistake as the enemy. Instead, they see it as an ordinary part of life they must overcome. That is true in any endeavor. As musicologist Eloise Ristad said, "When we give ourselves permission to fail, we at the same time give ourselves permission to excel."

5. UNDERSTAND THAT SETBACKS ARE USUALLY TEMPORARY

There's an old saying in Texas: "It doesn't matter how much milk you spill as long as you don't lose your cow." In other words, most mistakes, setbacks, and stumbles are not irreversible. As leaders, we must keep this in perspective. The problems come when you see only the spilled

> **"THE FELLOW WHO NEVER MAKES A MISTAKE TAKES HIS ORDERS FROM ONE WHO DOES."—HERBERT V. PROCHNOW**

milk and not the bigger picture. People who see adversity correctly take it in stride.

Mistakes don't make them want to give up.

Success doesn't make them think they've been set up.

Every event—good or bad—is just one small step in the process of living. Or as someone has said, "If silly things were not done, intelligent things would never happen."[4]

6. CONFESS THAT MISTAKES ARE NOT A SIGN OF WEAKNESS

Mistakes are not permanent markers. I love the perspective of the late poet Edwin Markham. In his poem "Victory in Defeat" he wrote,

> Defeat may serve as well as victory
> to shake the soul and let the glory out.

That's the way we need to look at adversity.

When you make mistakes, don't let them get you down. And don't let yourself think of them as a stigma. Turn adversity and the positive way you handle it a step toward success.

"DEFEAT MAY SERVE AS WELL AS VICTORY TO SHAKE THE SOUL AND LET THE GLORY OUT."—EDWIN MARKAHM

7. ADMIT THAT FAILURE IS NEITHER FATAL NOR FINAL

Even what may appear to be a huge failure doesn't need to keep you from leading your team well and fulfilling your greater goals. Take a look at the story of Sergio Zyman. He was the mastermind behind New Coke, something that marketing consultant Robert McMath saw as one of the greatest product failures of all time.[5] Zyman, who had previously introduced Diet Coke with great success, believed that Coca-Cola needed to act boldly to reverse its twenty-year market decline against its rival, Pepsi. His solution was to stop offering the drink that had been popular for nearly one hundred years, change the formula, and offer it as New Coke in 1985. The move was an abysmal failure that lasted seventy-nine days and cost the company about $100 million. People hated New Coke. And it caused Zyman to leave the company.

Years later, when asked if the venture was a mistake, Zyman answered, "No, categorically."

A failure? "No."

A blunder, a misstep, a bust?

"Another word between 'bust' and, uh, something else," Zyman replied. "Now if you say to me, 'The strategy that you guys embarked on didn't work,' I'll say, 'Yeah, absolutely it didn't work.' But the totality of the action ended up being positive."[6] Ultimately the return of Coca-Cola Classic made the company stronger.

IT'S ALL IN HOW YOU LOOK AT IT

If you tend to focus on the extremes of success and failure and to fixate on particular events in your life, try to put things into perspective. When you do, you'll be able to share the philosophy of someone like the apostle Paul, who was able to say, "I have learned in whatever state I am, to be content."[7] And that was saying a lot considering Paul was shipwrecked, whipped, beaten, stoned, and imprisoned. Despite these events, he remained resilient, he maintained perspective, and his faith was strong. He realized that as long as he was doing what he was supposed to, the labels of *success* or *failure* by others didn't matter.

Every person's life is filled with adversity, errors, and negative experiences. But know this:

ADVERSITY LEADS TO ERRORS
when we fail to be resilient.

ERRORS BECOME MISTAKES
when we perceive them and respond to them incorrectly.

MISTAKES BECOME FAILURE
if we *continually* respond to them incorrectly.

Becoming resilient means seeing errors and negative experiences as a regular part of life, learning from them, and bouncing back. By being resilient and perseverant, you can achieve your purpose in life. As essayist and short-story author Washington Irving once commented, "Great minds have purposes, others have wishes. Little minds are tamed and subdued by misfortunes; but great minds rise above them."

BECOMING RESILIENT MEANS SEEING ERRORS AND NEGATIVE EXPERIENCES AS A REGULAR PART OF LIFE, LEARNING FROM THEM, AND BOUNCING BACK.

The truth is that all roads to achievement must pass through the land of adversity. It has stood firmly between every human being who had a dream and the realization of that dream. The good news is that anyone can make it through adversity. We just need to remember that the process is not going to be easy. The problem is that we often get the wrong idea about that:

> Failure is really a matter of conceit. People don't work hard because, in their conceit, they imagine they'll succeed without ever making an effort. Most people believe that they'll wake up some day and find themselves rich. Actually, they've got it half right, because eventually they do wake up.[8]

Each of us has to make a choice. Are we going to sleep life away, avoiding adversity at all costs? Or are we going to wake up and realize this: *Adversity is simply a price we pay to achieve success.* If we learn to embrace that attitude toward adversity, then we are free to start moving ahead. And taking our team there.

ADVERSITY IS SIMPLY A PRICE WE PAY TO ACHIEVE SUCCESS.

CHAPTER 2

TRANSFORM TROUBLE INTO RESILIENCE

Business professors Gary Hamel and C. K. Prahalad have written about an interesting experiment. Four monkeys were placed in a room that had a tall pole in the center. Suspended from the top of that pole was a bunch of bananas. One of the hungry monkeys started climbing the pole to get something to eat, but just as he reached out to grab a banana, he was doused with a torrent of cold water. Squealing, he scampered down the pole and abandoned his attempt to feed himself. Each monkey made a similar attempt, and each one was drenched with cold water. After making several attempts, they finally gave up.

Then researchers removed one of the monkeys from the room and replaced him with a new monkey. As the newcomer began to climb the pole, the other three grabbed him and pulled him down to the ground.

After trying to climb the pole several times and being dragged down by the others, he finally gave up and never attempted to climb the pole again.

The researchers replaced the original monkeys, one by one, and each time a new monkey was brought in, he would be dragged down by the others before he could reach the bananas. In time, the room was filled with monkeys who had never received a cold shower. None of them would climb the pole, but not one of them knew why.[1]

DON'T LET ADVERSITY MAKE A MONKEY OUT OF YOU

Many days as leaders, we feel like one of those monkeys. We face adversity both internal and external, and it makes working tough. It makes leading even tougher. We try something new, and we get cold water dumped on our ideas. We try to accomplish a task, and members of the team drag us down. We have a hard time initiating change, and we're not even sure why. And like those monkeys, we become tempted to simply give up and give in to the status quo. Or worse, we become cynical and rigid.

What's the answer to this dilemma? Transform trouble into resilience. Accept adversity as normal, learn how to deal with it positively, and use it to develop a resilience that makes you better. Once you can handle trouble with grace and skill, you can lead your team to do the same.

LIFE IS FULL OF MESS UPS

Let's face it. Life is full of mess ups. We all face adversity, make mistakes, create failures, experience misfortunes, and face bad luck. What are we going to do when these things happen? Are we going to be defensive and rigid? Or are we going to be teachable and resilient? Rigid leaders make excuses, blame others, and fail to learn or grow.

But as I noted earlier, resilient leaders take responsibility, learn from adversity, and bounce back better than before.

Many years ago I came across a group of explanations that were said to be real from drivers describing auto accidents they were involved in:

"As I reached an intersection, a hedge sprang up, obscuring my vision."

"An invisible car came out of nowhere, struck my car, and vanished."

"The telephone pole was approaching fast. I attempted to swerve out of its path when it struck my front end."

"The indirect cause of this accident was a little guy in a small car with a big mouth."

"I had been driving my car for four years when I fell asleep at the wheel and had an accident."

"I was on the way to the doctor's with rear-end trouble when my universal joint gave way, causing me to have an accident."

"To avoid hitting the bumper of the car in front, I struck the pedestrian."

"I was coming home, pulled into the wrong driveway, and hit a tree I did not have."

"I was just keeping up with the cars behind me."

"The pedestrian had no idea which direction to run, so I ran over him."

"The guy was all over the road, and I had to swerve a number of times before hitting him."

"I pulled away at the side of the road, glanced at my mother-in-law, and headed over the embankment."[2]

How well would you say those drivers were doing at taking responsibility for their mess ups?

RIGID LEADERS MAKE EXCUSES, BLAME OTHERS, AND FAIL TO LEARN OR GROW. RESILIENT LEADERS TAKE RESPONSIBILITY, LEARN FROM ADVERSITY, AND BOUNCE BACK BETTER THAN BEFORE.

HOW NOT TO DEAL WITH ADVERSITY

Good leaders handle trouble well and grow in resilience as a result. Rigid leaders don't. Instead of navigating diversity well, when they face trouble, they do one of the following:

RIGID LEADERS BLOW UP

One of the reactions to adversity that limits people is anger. You've probably seen it. People make a minor mistake and angrily overreact to it, taking out their frustration on themselves or others around them.

Unchecked anger makes a small problem bigger. Nineteenth-century English author Charles Buxton said, "Bad temper is its own scourge. Few things are more bitter than to feel bitter. A man's venom poisons himself more than his victim." If people don't govern their temper, it will govern and limit them. People don't follow angry leaders; they fear them.

RIGID LEADERS COVER UP

It's in the nature of people to try to cover up their mistakes. That tendency is as old as Adam and Eve in the garden of Eden. And the results of a cover-up are as successful today as they were back then.

PEOPLE DON'T FOLLOW ANGRY LEADERS.

I recently heard a joke about a young navy pilot on maneuvers that shows how people often react to their mistakes. Prior to takeoff, the commanding admiral had ordered absolute radio silence from everyone engaged in the exercise. But one pilot mistakenly turned on his radio and was heard to mutter, "Boy am I fouled up!"

The admiral grabbed the mike from a radio operator and said, "Will the pilot who broke the radio silence identify himself immediately?"

There was a long silence. Finally a voice was heard over the radio: "I may be fouled up, but I'm not *that* fouled up!"

People's desire that others don't see their mistakes

isn't always so humorous. For example, take the case of Nicholas Leeson. In 1995 the twenty-eight-year-old worked for the British bank Barings. He controlled huge amounts of money for the organization, which he tried to increase through what's been called "casino-style" investing. When Leeson's dealings resulted in huge losses, he covered them up and made even riskier trades to try to recoup his losses. Analysts said it was like betting double or nothing in a gambling game. The problem was that Leeson kept coming up with nothing, creating bigger and bigger losses. Ultimately, his actions cost Barings $1.3 *billion*. He singlehandedly put one of the oldest banks in the world out of business.[3]

H. Stanley Judd said, "Don't waste energy trying to cover up failure. Learn from your failures and go on to the next challenge. It's OK to fail. If you're not failing, you're not growing." And if you're not bouncing back from failure, you're not becoming resilient.

RIGID LEADERS SPEED UP

People who are particularly stubborn will sometimes try to leave their troubles behind by working harder and faster, but without changing their direction. They're like the person trying to get the square peg in the round hole who first tries to place the peg in the hole, then tries to shove it in, then takes a hammer and tries to pound it in. They're working hard but not getting anywhere.

William Dean Singleton, co-owner of MediaNews Group Inc., said, "Too many people, when they make a mistake, just keep stubbornly plowing ahead and end up repeating the same mistakes. I believe in the motto, 'Try and try again.' But the way I read it, it says, 'Try, then stop and think. Then try again.'"

RIGID LEADERS REFUSE TO BACK UP

Have you ever been talking with someone who made a thoughtless remark during a conversation, and as soon as they said it, you could tell they knew they had made a mistake? Yet, they refused to admit it—even when someone called them on it? No matter what was said, instead of going back and apologizing, they justified the remark. All that did was make them more rigid, and as a result they never learn. They simply became more rigid.

When my wife, Margaret, and I were raising our

children, Elizabeth and Joel Porter (both of whom are now married with children of their own), we found that our son had a very strong will. When he did something wrong, his first move was to lie. Then he'd try to cover it up instead of backing up and apologizing. I can still picture his offended expression as he emphatically denied having eaten the chocolate candy, his nine-year-old face smeared with chocolate. Margaret and I worked very hard to help him break that inclination.

"DON'T WASTE ENERGY TRYING TO COVER UP FAILURE. LEARN FROM YOUR FAILURES AND GO ON TO THE NEXT CHALLENGE."—H. STANLEY JUDD

It has been said that a good man will stick up for what he believes is right, but it takes an even bigger man to quickly admit when he's in the wrong.[4] I'm relieved that today my boy Joel is a man I not only love but also respect and admire. When he's wrong, he admits it. And he has become quite resilient.

RIGID LEADERS EVENTUALLY GIVE UP

If you remain rigid in the face of adversity, you eventually *slow up*. And ultimately, you become tempted to *give up*. Being rigid and pretending you're right all the time is exhausting. Nobody is right all the time. Nobody avoids messes. Putting on a brave face and projecting perfection takes an extraordinary amount of energy. No wonder personal growth expert Paul J. Meyer said, "Ninety percent of all those who fail are not actually defeated. They simply quit." How much better would it be to be honest about our predicaments, deal with them authentically, and learn to roll with the punches?

"TRY, THEN STOP AND THINK. THEN TRY AGAIN."—WILLIAM DEAN SINGLETON

"NINETY PERCENT OF ALL THOSE WHO FAIL ARE NOT ACTUALLY DEFEATED. THEY SIMPLY QUIT."—PAUL J. MEYER

RESILIENT LEADERS BOUNCE BACK UP

The best way to deal with adversity as a leader is to transform trouble into resilience. When you make a mistake, put your team in a predicament, or create a problem, start by uttering some of the three most difficult words any leader can say: "I was wrong." You must open your eyes, admit your mistakes, and accept complete responsibility for any wrong actions you've taken and attitude you've exhibited. Every failure you experience is a fork in the road. It's an opportunity to take the right action, learn from your mistakes, bounce back, and begin again.

Leadership expert Peter Drucker says, "The better a man is, the more mistakes he will make, for the more new things he will try. I would never promote to a top-level job a man who was not making mistakes . . . otherwise he is sure to be mediocre." Mistakes really do pave the road to achievement.

MISTAKES PAVE THE ROAD TO ACHIEVEMENT.

Here is an acronym I created to help me keep mistakes in perspective. MISTAKES are . . .

Messages that give us feedback about life.
Interruptions that should cause us to reflect and think.
Signposts that direct us to the right path.
Tests that push us toward greater maturity.

Awakenings that keep us in the game mentally.
Keys that we can use to unlock the next door of opportunity.
Explorations that let us journey where we've never been before.
Statements about our development and progress.

"THE ONE QUALITY THAT ALL SUCCESSFUL PEOPLE HAVE IS THE ABILITY TO TAKE ON RESPONSIBILITY."—MICHAEL KORDA

Take full responsibility for yourself and your mistakes. As Michael Korda, former editor-in-chief of Simon and Schuster, said, "Success on any major scale requires you to accept responsibility. . . . In the final analysis, the one quality that all successful people have is the ability to take on responsibility."

The fight to take responsibility occurs within. And

talent, intelligence, or opportunity rarely make any difference in whether a person wins that battle. What does help is character. We must develop the will to do what's right in the face of wrong. We must find the grace to forgive our mistakes as well as those of others. We must cultivate the patience to learn. And we must dig deep for the fortitude to try again. These are first internal battles. That's why Stewart B. Johnson remarked, "Our business in life is not to get ahead of others, but to get ahead of ourselves—to break our own records, to outstrip our yesterday by our today."

"OUR BUSINESS IN LIFE IS NOT TO GET AHEAD OF OTHERS, BUT TO GET AHEAD OF OURSELVES–TO BREAK OUR OWN RECORDS, TO OUTSTRIP OUR YESTERDAY BY OUR TODAY."–STEWART B. JOHNSON

To win these internal battles, you must recognize the enemies of resilience and the self-sabotaging behavior that prevent the development of resilience. Fortunately, the next chapter will help you.

CHAPTER 3

AVOID THE ENEMIES OF RESILIENCE

When it comes to adversity, I have to agree with Jan Christian Smuts, a prime minister of South Africa in the first half of the twentieth century who desired to dismantle the country's apartheid system. He observed, "A man is not defeated by his opponents but by himself." Most leaders don't need to focus on overcoming their rivals. They need to learn how to get out of their own way. They need to develop internal skills to combat the enemies of resilience.

SELF-SABOTAGING BEHAVIORS THAT HINDER RESILIENCE

If you study people who fail to become resilient and have difficulty adapting, changing, growing, and improving, you will find that they often have several negative things in common. I've observed eight enemies of resilience that leaders would be wise to avoid if they want to lead their teams well, especially in our current challenging times. What are these behaviors?

1. EXPECTING TO FAIL

The law of human behavior says, "Sooner or later we will get what we expect." Usually, the people who succumb to adversity and keep failing are the ones who expect to. They're like the pessimist whose tombstone epitaph reads, "I expected this."

"SOONER OR LATER WE WILL GET WHAT WE EXPECT."—THE LAW OF HUMAN BEHAVIOR

In her autobiography, actress Helen Hayes wrote about the Thanksgiving when she cooked her first turkey. Before serving it, she made an announcement to her husband and son.

"Now I know this is the first turkey I've ever cooked," she said. "If it isn't any good, I don't want anybody to say a word. We'll just get up from the table, without comment, and go out to a restaurant to eat."

Hayes then went back to the kitchen to get the turkey. When she returned to the dining room, she found her husband and son seated at the table—with their hats and coats on.[1]

People cannot perform in a way inconsistent with the way they see themselves. Everybody fails. But people who continually expect to fail start seeing themselves as failures. And that leads to discouragement, not resilience. There's a big difference between failing and believing you are a failure.

2. TAKING ADVERSITY PERSONALLY

Oliver Goldsmith was born the son of a poor preacher in Ireland in the 1700s. Growing up, he wasn't a great student. His schoolmaster labeled him a "stupid blockhead." He did manage to earn a college degree, but he finished at the bottom of his class. He tried to become a preacher, but it didn't suit him. He tried law but failed at it. He settled on medicine, but he was an indifferent doctor. He lived in poverty, was often ill, and once even had to pawn his clothes to buy food.

PEOPLE CANNOT PERFORM IN A WAY INCONSISTENT WITH THE WAY THEY SEE THEMSELVES.

But then he discovered an interest and aptitude for writing. He took work as a Fleet Street reviewer and writer. Later, he began to write works that came out of his own interests. He secured his reputation as a novelist with *The Vicar of Wakefield*, a poet with "The Deserted Village," and a playwright with *She Stoops to Conquer*. In his lifetime, instead of taking his failures personally, he allowed adversity to make him better. After his death, he became a respected author in the British literary canon whose works are still studied today.

At the time we're making mistakes, it can be natural to take them personally. Try not to. Instead, think of them as "the kiss of Jesus," which was Mother Teresa's term for failures that drive us to God. Even doing what is *not* right for us can lead us to what we ought to be doing instead.

Sportswriter Grantland Rice observed, "Failure isn't so bad if it doesn't attack the heart. Success is all right if it doesn't go to the head." If you want to remain resilient, don't take your failures—or your successes—too personally. Remember, neither your failures nor successes have to define you.

3. REFUSING TO TAKE SMART RISKS

Life means risk. People who sabotage themselves shouldn't worry about failure as much as they should be concerned about the chances they miss when they are afraid to try. Speechwriter Charles Parnell observed,

"FAILURE ISN'T SO BAD IF IT DOESN'T ATTACK THE HEART. SUCCESS IS ALL RIGHT IF IT DOESN'T GO TO THE HEAD."—GRANTLAND RICE

"Too many people are having what might be called 'near-life experiences.' They go through life bunting, so afraid of failure that they never try to win the big prizes, never knowing the thrill of hitting a home run or even taking a swing at one."[2]

English poet Christopher Logue wrote this:

> Come to the edge.
> We might fall.
> Come to the edge.
> It's too high!
> COME TO THE EDGE!
> And they came,
> and he pushed,
> And they flew.[3]

Those who fly always first get out on the edge. If you want to seize an opportunity, you must take a risk. If you want to grow, you must make mistakes. If you want to reach your potential, you will have to take chances. If you don't, you will be resigned to a life of fear, rigidity, and mediocrity. The people who don't make mistakes often end up regretting the safe life they lived. As someone has observed, "Most people think too small, aim too low, and quit too soon."[4]

LIFE MEANS RISK.

When it comes to the thing you love to do, the thing you were made to do, aim high. Maxwell Maltz, developer of psycho-cybernetics, says, "You are a champion in the art of living if you reach only 65 percent of your goals." Does that help you become more open to risk? I hope so. Fear and resilience don't go together.

IF YOU WANT TO REACH YOUR POTENTIAL, YOU WILL HAVE TO TAKE CHANCES.

4. FEELING DEFEATED BY ADVERSITY

After a particularly bad defeat, legendary baseball manager Casey Stengel remarked, "You gotta lose 'em sometimes. When you do, lose 'em right." Everybody experiences losses. But not everybody allows themselves to be stopped by those losses. We must prepare ourselves for adversity. We should train for it, preparing to bounce back from it when it occurs. As professional snooker player Steve Davis said, "It may not be your fault for being down, but it is your fault for not getting up."

People who succeed develop an attitude of tenacity. They refuse to quit, and they are determined not to let adversity defeat them. If you want to become a resilient leader and you desire to fulfill your dreams, achieve your goals, and live life to the fullest, that's the kind of attitude you need to cultivate.

5. LISTENING TO NEGATIVE SELF-TALK

A noted psychiatrist once remarked that the two saddest words in the human vocabulary are *if only*. He believed that people who get trapped in their failures spend their whole lives saying, "If only." "If only I had tried harder; if only I had been more kind to my kids; if only I had been more truthful; if only . . ." The way to correct that mindset is to change your vocabulary by substituting the words *next time*—"Next time I will try harder; next time I will be more kind to my kids; next time I will be more truthful."

STEVE DAVIS SAID, "IT MAY NOT BE YOUR FAULT FOR BEING DOWN, BUT IT IS YOUR FAULT FOR NOT GETTING UP."

Adversity won't lead to failure if you do better the next time. In *Leaders on Leadership,* Warren Bennis interviewed seventy of the nation's top performers in numerous fields. None of them used the word *failure* to describe their mistakes. Instead they referred to learning experiences, tuition paid, detours, or opportunities for growth.[5] They knew how to talk positively to themselves.

6. LOSING YOUR SENSE OF HUMOR

One of the best things you can do for yourself when you make a mistake, experience bad luck, or fail is to laugh. I love the comment made by a humorist who said he spoke for an organization where they always rated the previous meeting's speaker in their program using little bells. Speakers who received a standing ovation got four bells next to their name. Those who were above average got three. Merely average speakers got two bells, and poor speakers got one. The humorist said that when he spoke to them several months ago, they awarded him the no-bell prize.

There isn't a person alive who wouldn't benefit from a good laugh, especially when they've done something really stupid or faced a difficult predicament. When you take yourself and what you do too seriously, then everything feels like life and death. When you feel that way and you face adversity, you sure die a lot. The way to solve that is to keep your sense of humor no matter how bad things get.

ADVERSITY WON'T LEAD TO FAILURE IF YOU DO BETTER THE NEXT TIME.

7. FAILING TO LEARN FROM MISTAKES

Successful restaurateur and celebrity chef Wolfgang Puck said, "I learned more from the one restaurant that didn't work than from all the ones that were successes." Isn't that usually the way it is? I know that I've learned more from my failures than from my successes—when I've remained teachable. When I didn't try to make excuses or place the blame on others, I always learned. That's why I loved a quote from Robert Kiyosaki, author of *Rich Dad, Poor Dad*. He said, "Sometimes you win and sometimes you learn." In fact, I loved it so much I wrote a book titled *Sometimes You Win, Sometimes You Learn.* Resilient leaders are determined to become learners, not losers, when they make mistakes, create messes, suffer setbacks, and face challenges, even when they are of their own making.

8. LOSING YOUR PERSPECTIVE

When ethicist and theologian Reinhold Niebuhr prayed the now famous "Serenity Prayer," he was preaching in a little church in Massachusetts. Only a small group of people was in the audience that day, but one person liked the prayer and after the service asked him for a copy.

"Here," Niebuhr responded, handing over a crumpled piece of paper. "I doubt I'll have any more use for it."

That simple prayer went on to become the most published prayer in America, and Alcoholics Anonymous adopted it.[6] It's ironic that Niebuhr's prayer became so popular. Evidently his perspective wasn't good because he didn't know what he had.

When football Hall of Fame coach Don Shula was head coach of the Miami Dolphins, he worked hard to keep his teams resilient and help them maintain perspective. How did he do that? He enforced a twenty-four-hour rule. He allowed himself, his players, and his coaches only twenty-four hours after a game to celebrate a victory or lament a loss. Once the twenty-four hours had passed, it was time to think about getting ready for the next game. That kind of perspective made Shula one of the most successful coaches in NFL history.

"I LEARNED MORE FROM THE ONE RESTAURANT THAT DIDN'T WORK THAN FROM ALL THE ONES THAT WERE SUCCESSES."—WOLFGANG PUCK

Psychologist Joyce Brothers observed, "The person interested in success has to learn to view failure as a healthy, inevitable part of the process of getting to the top." That's the right perspective.

To summarize: For becoming a resilient leader, you

need to put yourself in the best place you can to weather adversity. That starts with avoiding the enemies of resilience. You need to stay away from the kinds of negative beliefs that discourage you or make you feel defeated when you face trouble. You need to avoid patterns of thinking that make you believe you're a failure. You need to keep clear of attitudes that prevent you from getting back up when you get knocked down or stop you from learning and growing after a setback.

"THE PERSON INTERESTED IN SUCCESS HAS TO LEARN TO VIEW FAILURE AS A HEALTHY, INEVITABLE PART OF THE PROCESS OF GETTING TO THE TOP."—JOYCE BROTHERS

Resilient leaders learn to see failure as a friend, a companion to success. As actor Mickey Rooney said, "You always pass failure on the way to success." That means adversity can actually be an asset. It has value to you as a person and a leader. And that's what we'll be discussing in the next chapter.

CHAPTER 4

EMBRACE THE VALUE OF ADVERSITY

Human beings naturally tend toward inertia, but the successful life is an uphill journey. That's why self-improvement is such a struggle. It takes tremendous effort to keep climbing, growing, and improving. And that must be sustained while experiencing challenges. That's a reason adversity lies at the heart of every success. The process of achievement comes through repeated failures and the constant struggle to climb to a higher level.

When it comes to facing failure, most people will grudgingly concede that any person must make it through some adversity in order to succeed. They'll acknowledge that you must experience the occasional setback to make progress. But I believe that success comes only if you take that thought one step further. To achieve your dreams, you must *embrace* adversity and make failure a regular part of your life. If you're not failing, you're probably not really moving forward.

THE BENEFITS OF ADVERSITY

It may sound ironic, but if you have experienced a lot of adversity, you are actually in a better position to achieve success than people who haven't. When you fail, and fail, and fail again—and keep getting back up on your feet and keep learning from your failures—you are building strength, tenacity, experience, wisdom, and resilience. And people who develop such qualities can sustain their success, unlike many for whom good things come early and easily. So if you've failed a lot, celebrate. As long as you don't give up, you're in a very good place.

ADVERSITY LIES AT THE HEART OF EVERY SUCCESS. THE PROCESS OF ACHIEVEMENT COMES THROUGH REPEATED FAILURES AND THE CONSTANT STRUGGLE TO CLIMB TO A HIGHER LEVEL.

We may not like to think about it, but the benefits of adversity are many. Take a look at some of the key reasons you should embrace adversity and persevere through it to become a better leader:

1. ADVERSITY CREATES RESILIENCE

In the mid-1980s, *Time* magazine described a study of people who had lost their jobs three times due to plant closings. Psychologists were amazed by what they discovered. They expected the people who had been laid off to be beaten down and discouraged. Instead, they found them to be incredibly resilient. Why was that?

They concluded that people who had weathered repeated adversity had learned to bounce back. People who had lost a job and found a new one twice before were much better prepared to deal with adversity than someone who had always worked at the same place and had never faced adversity.[1]

WHEN YOU FAIL, AND FAIL, AND FAIL AGAIN— AND KEEP GETTING BACK UP ON YOUR FEET AND KEEP LEARNING FROM YOUR FAILURES— YOU ARE BUILDING STRENGTH, TENACITY, EXPERIENCE, WISDOM, AND RESILIENCE.

Nothing in life breeds resilience like adversity and failure. You've probably heard the popular phrase "Whatever doesn't kill you makes you stronger." That is certainly true if the challenges are beyond your ability to cope. The greater the adversity and the more frequent, the greater the potential for developing resilience.

2. ADVERSITY DEVELOPS MATURITY

Adversity can make you better if you don't let it make you bitter. Why? Because it promotes wisdom and maturity. American novelist William Saroyan said, "Good people are good because they've come to wisdom through failure. We get very little wisdom from success, you know."

NOTHING IN LIFE BREEDS RESILIENCE LIKE ADVERSITY AND FAILURE.

As the world continues to change at a faster and faster rate, maturity with flexibility becomes increasingly important. Those qualities come from weathering difficulties. Harvard Business School professor John Kotter said, "I can imagine a group of executives twenty years ago discussing a candidate for a top job and saying, 'This guy had a big failure when he was thirty-two.' Everyone else would say, 'Yep, yep, that's a bad sign.' I can imagine that same group considering a candidate today and saying, 'What worries me about this guy is that he's never failed.'"[2] The problems we face and overcome prepare our hearts for future difficulties.

3. ADVERSITY PROVIDES GREATER OPPORTUNITIES

I believe that eliminating problems limits our potential. Just about every successful entrepreneur I've met has numerous stories of adversity and setbacks that opened doors to greater opportunity for them. For example, in 1978, Bernie Marcus, the son of a poor Russian cabinetmaker in Newark, New Jersey, was fired from Handy Dan, a do-it-yourself hardware retailer. That prompted Marcus to team with Arthur Blank to start their own business. In 1979 they opened their first store in Atlanta, Georgia. It was called Home Depot. Today, Home Depot has over two thousand stores, they have expanded the business to include overseas operations, and each year they do more than $159 billion in sales.[3]

THE PROBLEMS WE FACE AND OVERCOME PREPARE OUR HEARTS FOR FUTURE DIFFICULTIES.

I'm sure Bernie Marcus wasn't very happy about getting fired from his job at Handy Dan all those years ago. But if he hadn't been, who knows whether he would have achieved the success he later did co-founding and leading Home Depot, nor would he have achieved the many philanthropic initiatives he accomplished in his lifetime.

4. ADVERSITY PROMPTS INNOVATION

Early in the twentieth century, a boy whose family had immigrated from Sweden to Illinois sent twenty-five cents to a publisher for a book on photography. What he received instead was a book on ventriloquism. What did he do? He adapted and learned ventriloquism. His name was Edgar Bergen, and for more than forty years he entertained audiences with the help of a wooden dummy named Charlie McCarthy.

The ability to innovate is at the heart of creativity—a vital component in success. Often, that comes from resilience. University of Houston professor Jack Matson recognized that fact and developed a course that his students came to call "Failure 101." In it, Matson had students build mock-ups of products that no one would ever buy. His goal was to get students to equate failure with innovation instead of defeat. That way they would increase their creativity and be freed up to try new things. They therefore learn, says Matson, "to reload and get ready to shoot again." If you want to succeed, you must learn to adjust the way you do things and keep trying. That comes from being resilient in the face of adversity and adapting to conditions.

5. ADVERSITY BRINGS UNEXPECTED BENEFITS

The average person makes a mistake and automatically thinks that it's a failure. But some of the greatest stories of success can be found in the unexpected benefits of mistakes. For example, most people are familiar with the story of Edison and the phonograph. He discovered it while trying—and failing—to invent something entirely different. But did you also know that Kellogg's Corn Flakes resulted when boiled wheat was left in a baking pan overnight? Or that Ivory soap floats because a batch was left in the mixer too long and a large volume of air was whipped into it? Or that the product Scott Towels was launched when a toilet paper machine put too many layers of tissue together? These are all situations where something "went wrong" and led to something right.

Horace Walpole said that "in science, mistakes always precede the truth." That's what happened to German-Swiss chemist Christian Friedrich Schönbein. One day he was in the kitchen—which his wife had strictly forbidden—experimenting with sulfuric and nitric acid. When he accidentally spilled some of the mixture on the kitchen table, he thought he was in trouble. (He *knew* he would experience "adversity" when his wife found out!) He hurriedly snatched up a cotton apron, wiped up the mess, and hung the apron by the fire to dry.

Suddenly there was a violent explosion. Evidently the cellulose in the cotton underwent a process called "nitration." Unwittingly, Schönbein had invented nitrocellulose—what came to be called smokeless gunpowder or guncotton. He went on to market his invention, which made him a fortune.

So often when we face adversity, all we can see is what went wrong. Resilient leaders acknowledge what's wrong, but also look for what's right. They search for any benefit they can find in a failure, and they try to make the most of it.

6. ADVERSITY MOTIVATES

A story is told about legendary Alabama football coach Bear Bryant, in a game years ago when his Crimson Tide team was ahead by six points with less than two minutes remaining in the game. Bryant sent in his quarterback with instructions to play it safe and run out the clock.

In the huddle the quarterback said, "Coach says to play it safe, but that's what they're expecting. Let's give them a surprise." And with that, he called a pass play.

RESILIENT LEADERS ACKNOWLEDGE WHAT'S WRONG, BUT ALSO LOOK FOR WHAT'S RIGHT.

When the quarterback dropped back and threw the pass, the defending cornerback, who was a champion sprinter, intercepted the ball and headed toward the end zone expecting to score a touchdown. The quarterback, who was not known as a good runner, took off after the cornerback and ran him down from behind! He tackled him on the five-yard line, preventing a touchdown and saving the game.

After the clock ran out, the opposing coach approached Bear Bryant and said, "What's this business about your quarterback not being a runner? He ran down my speedster from behind!"

Bryant responded, "Your man was running for six points. My man was running for his life."

Nothing can motivate a person like adversity. Olympic diver Pat McCormick says, "I think failure is one of the great motivators. After my narrow loss in the

1948 trials, I knew how really good I could be. It was the defeat that focused all my concentration on my training and goals." McCormick went on to win two gold medals in the Olympics in London that year and another two in Helsinki four years later.

If you can step back from the negative circumstances you face in life, you will be able to discover that there are positive benefits to your negative experiences. That is almost always true; you simply have to be willing to look for them. So if you lose your job, think about not only the resilience you're developing but the greater doors of opportunity that may be opening before you. If you find yourself in a difficult predicament and must try something daring and you survive, think about what adversity taught you about yourself—and how it can help you take on new challenges. If you order a book like Edgar Bergen or sign up for an online course and it turns out to be different from what you wanted and expected, instead of seeing it as a loss, figure out if it's an opportunity to learn a new skill. As Bill Vaughan said, "In the game of life it's a good idea to have a few early losses, which relieves you of the pressure of trying to maintain an undefeated season." Those losses also teach you resilience.

"IN THE GAME OF LIFE IT'S A GOOD IDEA TO HAVE A FEW EARLY LOSSES, WHICH RELIEVES YOU OF THE PRESSURE OF TRYING TO MAINTAIN AN UNDEFEATED SEASON."—BILL VAUGHAN

To summarize: Experiencing adversity and failure doesn't mean you'll never succeed. It just means it may take longer than you expected, and you need to remain flexible along the way. John Wayne uttered a great line in the movie *The Train Robbers* that provides great advice as we work to remain resilient: "You're going to spend the rest of your life getting up one more time than you're knocked down, so you'd better start getting used to it."

That's what success is—getting up one time more than you fall. And finding and embracing the advantages of adversity.

CHAPTER 5

HARNESS THE POWER OF RESILIENCE

What usually separates the best from the rest? Have you ever thought about that? What separates the gold medalist from the silver medalist in the Olympics? What separates the successful entrepreneur from the one who doesn't make it? What makes it possible for one person to thrive after a debilitating accident while another gives up and dies? It's resilience.

Sure, every now and then there are people like Mozart, someone whose gifts are so extraordinary that they can achieve things the rest of us can only dream of. (But even they are assisted by the possession of positive attitudes toward adversity.) Most people at the top of their professions are comparable when it comes to talent. Gold and silver medals are usually separated by only hundredths of seconds. Professional golfers play seventy-two holes in tournaments and often win by a single stroke. As Denis Waitley said in *The Winner's Edge,* "The winner's edge is not in a gifted birth, a high IQ, or in talent. The winner's edge is all in the attitude, not aptitude. Attitude is the criterion for success. But you can't buy an attitude for a million dollars. Attitudes are not for sale."[1]

"THE WINNER'S EDGE IS NOT IN A GIFTED BIRTH, A HIGH IQ, OR IN TALENT. THE WINNER'S EDGE IS ALL IN THE ATTITUDE, NOT APTITUDE."—DENIS WAITLEY

Resilience is a choice. For years I have tried to live by the following statement: I cannot always choose what happens to me, but I can always choose what happens in me. Some things in life are beyond my control. Some things are within it. I can choose to have a positive attitude in the face of adversity, look for the positives, learn from the negatives, decide to become better, and get back into the race. That is why I believe my attitude is either my biggest asset or greatest liability. It can make or break me. That is the same for you. Your attitude toward adversity will either lift you up or bring you down. It will lead to optimism and resilience or cynicism and rigidity.

WHAT RESILIENCE CAN DO FOR YOU

Resilience can be an asset every day in nearly every way. It not only helps with little issues, but it also provides a positive framework from which a person can approach all of life. Here's what I mean:

RESILIENCE IS A CHOICE.

1. RESILIENCE MAKES A DIFFERENCE IN YOUR APPROACH TO LIFE

A lot has been written about the men and women who survived the Depression and fought World War II, the people Tom Brokaw called "the greatest generation." I recall reading somewhere a story about a woman of that generation who followed her husband to a U.S. Army camp in the desert of Southern California during the war. The man had advised against it, thinking that she would be more comfortable back East with her family, but the young bride didn't want to be separated from her new husband.

The only living accommodation they could find was a run-down shack near a Native American village. The place was very basic. During the day, temperatures often reached 115 degrees. The wind, which blew constantly, felt like air from a furnace. And the dust made everything miserable.

The young woman found the days to be long and boring. Her only neighbors were Native Americans with whom she could find little in common. When her husband was sent into the desert for two weeks of maneuvers, she broke down. The living conditions and loneliness were too much for her. She wrote her mother to say that she wanted to come home. A short time later, she received a reply from home. One of the things her mother told her was this:

Two men looked through prison bars;
One saw mud; the other saw stars.

As the young woman read the lines over and over, she first felt ashamed. Then her resolve grew. So did her resilience. She truly wanted to stay with her husband, so she made a decision. She would look for the stars.

The next day, she worked to make friends with her neighbors. As she got to know them, she also asked them to teach her about their weaving and pottery. At first, they were reluctant. But as they saw that her interest in them and their work was genuine, they became more open. The more the woman learned about the Native American culture and history, the more she wanted to know. Her perspective started changing. Even the desert began to look different to her. She began to appreciate its quiet beauty, its tough but beautiful plants, and the rocks and fossilized seashells she found as she explored. She even began to write about her experiences there.

What had changed? Not the desert. Not the people who lived there. She had. Her attitude had transformed—and as a result, so did her outlook and her resilience.

The happiest people in life don't necessarily have the best of everything. They're resilient and try to make the best of everything. They're like the person in a remote village going to a well every day to get water who says, "Every time I come to this well, I come away with my bucket full!" instead of, "I can't believe I have to keep coming back to this well to fill up my bucket!"

A person's attitude and resulting resilience has a profound influence on his approach to life. Ask coaches before a big game whether their attitude and that of their players will make a difference in the outcome of the game. Ask surgeons if the patient's attitude matters when they are trying to save lives in an emergency room. Ask teachers if students' attitudes have an impact before they take a test. Resilience is choosing to believe you can be successful. It's choosing to accept adversity when it comes. It's choosing to make the best of it, bounce back, and try again.

THE HAPPIEST PEOPLE IN LIFE DON'T NECESSARILY HAVE THE BEST OF EVERYTHING. THEY'RE RESILIENT.

One of the things I've learned is that life often gives you whatever you expect from it. If you expect bad things, those are what you get. If you expect good things, you often receive them. I don't know why it works that way, but it does. If you don't believe me, try it out. Give yourself thirty days in which you expect the best of everything: the best parking place, the best table in the restaurant, the best interaction with clients, the best treatment from service people. You'll be surprised by what you encounter, especially if you give your very best to others in every situation as well.

2. RESILIENCE MAKES A DIFFERENCE IN YOUR RELATIONSHIPS WITH PEOPLE

Many years ago at a conference where I was speaking, I met Colleen Barrett, former president and corporate secretary for Southwest Airlines, in the greenroom. I was eager to talk with her because for many years while other airlines had lost money and struggled to survive, Southwest had succeeded and made a profit.

LIFE OFTEN GIVES YOU WHATEVER YOU EXPECT FROM IT.

Colleen and I talked leadership. One of the things that she said the company was most proud of was their reputation for great customer service. When I asked her how they accomplished it, she told me that the company didn't rely on a lot of rules. There were, of course, FAA regulations that they complied with, and they had rules requiring flight attendants to always be on time for their assignments since their staffing is lean. But the company's emphasis wasn't on procedures. It was on creating the right kind of attitude among employees. They wanted them to be flexible, creative, and resilient. Southwest's workers were empowered to evaluate situations and make decisions. And their focus was on people skills and the golden rule. Even when employees made mistakes, as long as they were attempting to see things from the customer's point of view and trying to give good service, they were supported.

It seems obvious to say, but to be successful, leaders need to be able to work well with others. Many factors come into play when it comes to people skills, but what makes or breaks that ability is a person's attitude. Even the best people person can find it challenging to work with others. If you can remain positive and resilient when interacting with others, you can go far.

IF YOU CAN REMAIN POSITIVE AND RESILIENT WHEN INTERACTING WITH OTHERS, YOU CAN GO FAR.

Some years ago I wrote a book called *Winning with People* in which I describe twenty-five people principles that anyone can use to become better at building relationships and working with others. Many of those principles are attitude-based. Here are some examples:

The Lens Principle: Who we are determines how we see others. Our perception of others depends more on our attitude than it does their characteristics. If we are positive, we see them as positive.

The Pain Principle: Hurting people hurt people and are easily hurt by them. Our negative experiences and emotional baggage color our perception of others' actions. Normal interactions can cause us pain even when another person did nothing to inflict pain.

The Elevator Principle: We can lift people up or

take them down in our relationships. People possess a mindset of either lifting or limiting others.

The Learning Principle: Each person we meet has the potential to teach us something. Some people possess a teachable attitude, and they assume that they can learn something from everyone they meet. Others look down on many people and assume that they have nothing to offer.

There are other attitude-based principles in the book, but you get the idea. When it comes to dealing with people, attitude makes a difference and resilience is essential. Why? Because working with people always brings challenges, conflict, problems, and adversity. If you're too rigid, the relationship can break. If you're resilient, it will bounce back.

IF YOU'RE TOO RIGID, THE RELATIONSHIP CAN BREAK. IF YOU'RE RESILIENT, IT WILL BOUNCE BACK.

If your track record of dealing with people isn't as good as you would like it to be, maybe you need to look at your attitude. While it's true that some people just seem to have a naturally winning way with others, even someone with limited natural people skills can learn to win with others if he decides to have a positive attitude toward people and become more flexible.

3. RESILIENCE MAKES A DIFFERENCE IN HOW YOU FACE CHALLENGES

It's said that when U.S. Marine Chesty Puller found himself surrounded by eight enemy divisions during the Korean War, his response was, "All right, they are on our left. They are on our right. They're in front of us. They're behind us—they can't get away from us this time!"

In life, obstacles, challenges, problems, and failures are inevitable. How are you going to handle them? Will you give up? Will you allow circumstances to make you miserable? Or will you be resilient and try to make the best of things? Which path you choose depends on your attitude.

I once heard a lecturer say that no society has ever developed tough people during times of peace. I believe that to be true. Think back to the times in your life when you have grown the most. I'm willing to bet that you grew as the result of overcoming difficulties. The more resilient you were, the more likely you were to be able to overcome difficulties, grow, and move forward.

You can see this pattern of resilience in the face of challenges in the lives of great men and women:

- Demosthenes, called the greatest orator of ancient Greece, possessed a speech impediment. Legend has it he overcame it by reciting verses with pebbles in his mouth and speaking over the roar of the waves at the seashore.
- Martin Luther, father of the Reformation, made use of the time he was confined in the castle of Wartburg to translate the New Testament into German.
- Composer Ludwig van Beethoven wrote his greatest symphonic masterpieces after he had become deaf.

- John Bunyan wrote *Pilgrim's Progress* while in prison.
- Daniel Defoe also wrote while in prison, producing *Robinson Crusoe.*

I've been told that in the Chinese language two words are often combined to create another word with a very different meaning. For example, when the symbol for the word meaning *man* is combined with the symbol for the word meaning *woman,* the resulting word means *good.*

EVERY CHALLENGE HAS AN OPPORTUNITY. AND EVERY OPPORTUNITY HAS A CHALLENGE.

Resilience can have a similar effect. When a problem comes into contact with someone possessing resilience, the result is often something wonderful. Out of the turmoil that problems cause can emerge great statesmen, scientists, authors, or businesspeople. Every challenge has an opportunity. And every opportunity has a challenge. Our level of resilience determines how we handle them.

4. RESILIENCE MAKES THE DIFFERENCE WHEN FACING TRAGEDY

When is resilience most important? When does it make the greatest difference? It's not during a sporting event or when business gets tough. It's when life itself is on the line. When I was a pastor, I spent much time with people dealing with tragedies. I've visited with a lot of patients before surgery, and the ones who did the best afterward and recovered the most quickly were the people who were resilient. I've visited many nursing homes. The elderly people who thrive are the ones who are still positive about themselves and their situation. I heard from a nursing home official that the new patients who feel like they were forced into nursing homes and had no other options tended to give up and die sooner than those who are resilient and see the move as just another phase of life to be met with positively.

Many people have written about the power of a

positive resilience on health and fitness. Many medical personnel say they have seen a positive correlation between people's attitudes and their ability to recover from illnesses such as cancer. Dr. Ernest H. Rosenbaum and Isadora R. Rosenbaum have reported how this observation leads to new studies:

> Researchers are now experimenting with methods of actively enlisting the mind in the body's combat with cancer. . . . Some doctors and psychologists now believe that the proper attitude may even have a direct effect on cell function and consequently may be used to arrest, if not cure, cancer. This new field of scientific study, called psychoneuroimmunology, focuses on the effect that mental and emotional activity has on physical well-being, indicating that patients can play a much larger role in their recovery.[2]

Seeing a connection between people's thoughts and feelings and their health is nothing new. Rosenbaum points out, "We have known for over 2,000 years—from the writings of Plato and Galen—that there is a direct correlation between the mind, the body and one's health."[3] Our choices make or break us. Poet John Milton wrote,

> The mind is its own place, and it itself
> Can make a heav'n of hell, a hell of heav'n.[4]

Your attitude has a profound influence on how you see the world—and thus on the way you live out your life. When you choose resilience, you harness its power for yourself, your loved ones, your team, and others.

CHAPTER 6

ADOPT THE HABITS OF RESILIENT LEADERS

Every successful person is someone who faced great adversity yet remained resilient in the face of it. For example, Wolfgang Mozart, one of the great geniuses of musical composition, was told by Emperor Ferdinand that his opera *The Marriage of Figaro* was "far too noisy" and contained "far too many notes." Artist Vincent van Gogh, whose paintings now set records for the sums they bring at auction, sold only one painting in his lifetime. Thomas Edison, the most prolific inventor in history, was considered unteachable. And Albert Einstein, the greatest thinker of our time, was told by a Munich school master that he would "never amount to much."

I think it's safe to say that all great achievers are given multiple reasons to believe they were failures and to quit. In spite of that, they persevered. In the face of adversity, rejection, and failings, they continued believing in themselves, they bounced back, and they went on to achieve great things.

EIGHT ABILITIES SHARED BY RESILIENT LEADERS

Like many people, you may have a hard time maintaining a positive mindset and remaining resilient in the face of life's challenges. But know this: It is possible no matter your circumstances or personal history. You can make choices that increase your resilience. Here are eight I encourage you to embrace to become a more resilient leader:

1. RESILIENT LEADERS REJECT REJECTION

Author James Allen stated, "A man is literally what he thinks, his character being the complete sum of all this thought." That's why it's important to make sure your thinking is on the right track, especially in the face of adversity, rejection, and failure.

"A MAN IS LITERALLY WHAT HE THINKS, HIS CHARACTER BEING THE COMPLETE SUM OF ALL THIS THOUGHT."—JAMES ALLEN

Psychologist Martin E. Seligman believed we have two choices when we fail. We can internalize or externalize our failure. "People who blame themselves when they fail . . . think they are worthless, talentless, unlovable," says Seligman. "People who blame external events do not lose self-esteem when bad events strike."[1]

The weight of failure, mistakes, and adversity can be crushing if you internalize it. It can cloud your judgment. If your focus is on condemning yourself when you make a mistake or experience a setback, you won't be able to effectively lead others. To keep the right perspective, take responsibility for your actions, but don't take failure too personally. Reject rejection before it threatens to take you down.

2. RESILIENT LEADERS SEE FAILURE AS TEMPORARY

People who personalize failure see a problem as a hole they're permanently stuck in. But resilient people see any predicament as temporary. For example, take the case of United States President Harry S. Truman. In 1922 he was thirty-eight years old, in debt, and out of work. In 1945 he was the most powerful leader of the free world occupying the highest office in the land. If he had seen failure as permanent, he would have remained stuck and never would have kept trying and believing in his potential.

Sometimes we need resilience to bounce back from

immediate difficulties. We need to remain flexible to overcome a challenge. We need resilience to remain positive in the midst of a setback. We need resilience to get through a sudden mess. But other times we need resilience for the long haul. We need to remain positive, flexible, and adaptable for months, years, or even decades before we see the results we desire.

TAKE RESPONSIBILITY FOR YOUR ACTIONS,
BUT DON'T TAKE FAILURE TOO PERSONALLY.

3. RESILIENT LEADERS SEE FAILURES AS ISOLATED INCIDENTS

Many years ago author Leo Buscaglia talked about his admiration for cooking icon Julia Child. He said, "I just love her attitude. She says, 'Tonight we're going to make a soufflé!' And she beats this and whisks that, and she drops things on the floor . . . and does all these wonderful human things. Then she takes the soufflé and throws it in the oven and talks to you for a while. Finally, she says, 'Now it's ready!' But when she opens the oven, the soufflé just falls flat as a pancake. But does she panic or burst into tears? No! She smiles and says, 'Well, you can't win them all. Bon appétit!'"

Resilience means seeing adversity as a temporary event, not a lifelong epidemic. Resilient leaders don't let challenges color everything they see or convince them that they can't achieve their goals. They don't take failure personally. They persevere through it.

4. RESILIENT LEADERS KEEP EXPECTATIONS REALISTIC

The greater the feat you desire to achieve, the greater the mental preparation to create resilience for overcoming obstacles and persevering over the long haul. If you want to take a stroll in your neighborhood, you can reasonably expect to have few if any problems. But that's not the case if you intend to climb Mount Everest. It takes time, effort, and the resiliency to overcome setbacks. You must approach each day with reasonable expectations and not get your feelings hurt when everything doesn't turn out perfectly.

RESILIENCE MEANS SEEING ADVERSITY AS A TEMPORARY EVENT.

Something that happened on baseball's opening day in 1954 illustrates the point well. The Milwaukee Braves and the Cincinnati Reds played one another, and a rookie for each team made their major league debuts during that game. The rookie who played for the Reds hit four doubles and helped his team win with a score of 9–8. The rookie for the Braves went 0 for 5. The Red's player was Jim Greengrass, a name you may have never heard. The other guy, who didn't get a hit, might be more familiar to you. His name was Hank Aaron, the player who became the best home run hitter in the history of baseball.

If Aaron's expectations for that first game had been

unrealistic, who knows, he might have given up baseball. Surely he wasn't happy about his performance that day, but he was resilient. He had worked too hard to get into the Majors, and he wasn't about to give up easily. He made 13,941 plate appearances in his twenty-two-year career, and had hit 755 home runs when he finished in 1976, a record at the time.

5. RESILIENT LEADERS FOCUS ON STRENGTHS

All good leaders focus on their strengths and those of their team members. Not only does that put everyone in the best position to succeed, but it also minimizes failure and maximizes resilience. Bob Butera, who served in the 1980s as president of the New Jersey Devils hockey team, was asked what makes a winner. He answered this way:

> What distinguishes winners from losers is that winners concentrate at all times on what they *can* do, not on what they can't do. If a guy is a great shooter but not a great skater, we tell him to think only about the shot, the shot, the shot—never about some other guy outskating him. The idea is to remember your successes.

"WHAT DISTINGUISHES WINNERS FROM LOSERS IS THAT WINNERS CONCENTRATE AT ALL TIMES ON WHAT THEY CAN DO, NOT ON WHAT THEY CAN'T DO."—BOB BUTERA

If a weakness is a matter of character, it needs attention. Focus on it until you shore it up. Otherwise, the best bet for success is to develop and maximize your strengths. It's the best way to start successfully and the best way to bounce back when overcoming adversity.

6. RESILIENT LEADERS VARY THEIR APPROACHES TO ACHIEVEMENT

In *The Psychology of Achievement,* Brian Tracy writes about four millionaires who made their fortunes by age thirty-five. They were involved in an average of *seventeen* businesses before finding the one that took them to the top. They kept trying and changing until they found something that worked for them. That's resilience!

People who are successful are willing to vary their approaches to problems. That's important in every walk of life, not just business. For example, if you're a fan of track-and-field events, you have undoubtedly enjoyed watching athletes compete in the high jump. I'm always amazed by the heights achieved by the men and women in those events. What's really interesting is that in the 1960s, the sport went through a major change in technique that allowed athletes to break the old records and push them up to new levels.

The person responsible for that change was Dick Fosbury. Where previous athletes used the straddle method to high jump, in which they went over the bar while facing it, with one arm and one leg leading, Fosbury developed a technique where he went over head first with his back to the bar. It was dubbed the "Fosbury flop."

Developing a new high jump technique was one thing. Getting people with rigid thinking to embrace it was another matter. Fosbury remarked, "I was told over and over again that I would never be successful, that I was not going to be competitive, and the technique was simply not going to work. All I could do was shrug and say, 'We'll just have to see.'"

And people did see. Fosbury won the gold medal in the Mexico City Olympics in 1968, shattering the previous Olympic record and setting a new world record in the process. Since then, nearly all world-class high jumpers use his technique. To achieve his goals, Fosbury varied his approach to high jumping, and he didn't allow others' lack of flexibility to defeat him.

7. RESILIENT LEADERS PRIORITIZE ACTION

One of the great benefits of having resilience is that it frees a leader to take action, while lack of resilience often causes a leader to become stuck in inaction. I've observed this often in people who lack flexibility. They can find themselves stuck because they are overwhelmed by one of these three conditions:

PARALYSIS

For some people, lack of resilience brings about paralysis. Because adversity creates so much fear in them, they simply stop trying to do anything because they worry it might lead to further failure. President Harry S. Truman said, "The worst danger we face is the danger of being paralyzed by doubts and fears. This danger is brought on by those who abandon faith and sneer at hope. It is brought on by those who spread cynicism and distrust and try to blind us to the great chance to do good for all mankind." People whose fear paralyzes them often give up any hope of moving forward.

"THE WORST DANGER WE FACE IS THE DANGER OF BEING PARALYZED BY DOUBTS AND FEARS."—HARRY S. TRUMAN

PROCRASTINATION

Other people maintain the hope of progress but simply never get around to following through. Someone once said that procrastination is fertilizer that makes difficulties grow. Victor Kiam stated it even more strongly: He

PROCRASTINATION IS FERTILIZER THAT MAKES DIFFICULTIES GROW.

called it opportunity's natural assassin.

Procrastination steals a person's time, productivity, and potential. As President John F. Kennedy said, "There are risks and costs to a program of action, but they are far less than the long-range risks and costs of comfortable inaction." Procrastination is too high a price to pay for fearing adversity.

PURPOSELESSNESS

Tom Peters, coauthor of *In Search of Excellence*, says there's nothing more useless than someone who comes to the end of the day and congratulates himself, saying,

"Well, I made it through the day without screwing up." Yet that's what many people who lack resilience do. Rather than pursuing worthy objectives, they avoid the pain of making mistakes. And because they possess that mindset, they lose sight of any sense of purpose that they might have once possessed.

Being resilient doesn't only mean being able to take a punch. It means having the ability to get back up again, try new approaches to success, and moving to keep from being punched again.

8. RESILIENT LEADERS BOUNCE BACK BETTER

One thing successful people have in common is the ability to bounce back after an error, mistake, or failure. Psychologist Simone Caruthers says, "Life is a series of outcomes. Sometimes the outcome is what you want. Great. Figure out what you did right. Sometimes the outcome is what you don't want. Great. Figure out what you did so you don't do it again."[2] That resilience is the key to bouncing back.

The bad news is that if your thinking and your actions have been rigid for a long time, and you're not used to taking action as a resilient leader, getting started may be difficult. The good news is that as soon as you start putting the habits of resilient leaders into action, it gets easier. If you take action and keep making mistakes, you gain experience and develop resilience. As President Teddy Roosevelt said, "He who makes no mistakes makes no progress."

Playwright George Bernard Shaw said, "A life spent in making mistakes is not only more honorable but more useful than a life spent doing nothing." To break the cycle of inaction, you must be willing to know that much of your life will be spent making mistakes and refuse to allow it to stop you from living your life, leading your team well, and being successful.

"A LIFE SPENT IN MAKING MISTAKES IS NOT ONLY MORE HONORABLE BUT MORE USEFUL THAN A LIFE SPENT DOING NOTHING."—GEORGE BERNARD SHAW

CHAPTER 7

TEACH YOUR TEAM TO TAKE ADVANTAGE OF ADVERSITY

When things go wrong, how do your team members react? Does it crush them? Or does it challenge them to do better? Their attitude toward adversity will determine their performance. Adversity can be your team members' friend or enemy. Adversity a friend? Yes. How? By learning how to benefit from it. Benjamin Franklin said, "The things which hurt, instruct." If you teach the members of your team to learn from their failures, mistakes, and setbacks, then they can actually turn adversity into advantage—and become more resilient in the process.

THEY MUST BE WILLING TO LEARN

"THE THINGS WHICH HURT, INSTRUCT."
—BENJAMIN FRANKLIN

A person's attitude after failure determines their teachability, and to some degree, indicates their level of resilience. Here's an example of what I mean. John H. Holliday, the founder and editor of the *Indianapolis News,* stormed out of his office one day in search of the person who had spelled *height* as *hight*. When a worker checked the original copy and explained that Holiday himself had been the one who did it, the editor's response was, "Well, if that's the way I spelled it, that has to be right." The paper misspelled the word his way for the next thirty years. As Louis Armstrong insightfully quipped, "There are some people that if they don't know, you can't tell them."

Teachability is an attitude, a mindset that says, "No matter how much I know (or think I know), I can learn from this situation." That kind of thinking can help you turn adversity into advantage. It can make your team a winner even during the most difficult of circumstances. Sydney Harris says, "A winner knows how much he still has to learn, even when he is considered an expert by others. A loser wants to be considered an expert by others before he has learned enough to know how little he knows."

"THERE ARE SOME PEOPLE THAT IF THEY DON'T KNOW, YOU CAN'T TELL THEM."—LOUIS ARMSTRONG

"A WINNER KNOWS HOW MUCH HE STILL HAS TO LEARN, EVEN WHEN HE IS CONSIDERED AN EXPERT BY OTHERS."—SYDNEY HARRIS

HOW TO HELP YOUR TEAM LEARN FROM FAILURES AND MISTAKES

How can you help your team to adopt this kind of mindset? Convince them they can take advantage of adversity, and then show them how to do it. Journalist William Bolitho Ryall said, "The most important thing in life is not to capitalize on our gains. Any fool can do that. The most important thing is to profit from your losses. That requires intelligence; and it makes the difference between a man of sense and a fool."

To turn losses into profits, have your team members ask the following questions every time they deal with adversity:

1. WHAT CAUSED THE FAILURE?

You cannot find out what you can do right unless you do all you can to find out what went wrong. So that's where they need to start. Start by challenging them to examine the problem and result by asking:

What happened?
Where did things break down?
Was there a clear point where we went off course?
Did we make a mistake?
Was there a timing issue?

People can't learn from failure if they fail to identify the cause of a problem.

"THE MOST IMPORTANT THING IS TO PROFIT FROM YOUR LOSSES."
—WILLIAM BOLITHO RYALL

---

2. WAS THE RESULT A FAILURE, OR DID WE JUST FALL SHORT?

The next thing they need to do is determine if what happened was really a failure. What we think is our fault could have been an attempt to fulfill unrealistic expectations.

Before he retired from office, President Ronald Reagan told a story about *Three Musketeers* author Alexandre Dumas. The novelist and a friend had a terrible argument, and it got so heated that one challenged the other to a duel. Both Dumas and his friend were expert marksmen, and they feared that if they proceeded with the duel, both of them would die. So they decided to draw straws to determine which of them would shoot himself. Dumas picked the short straw.

With a sigh, he picked up his pistol, walked into the library, and closed the door, leaving behind him a group of worried friends. After a few moments, the loud report of a pistol shot echoed from the library. His friends immediately charged into the room, and there stood Dumas with the pistol still smoking in his hand.

"An amazing thing just happened," said Dumas. "I missed."

Whether we put unrealistic expectation on ourselves or someone else did, if a goal is unrealistic and the team misses it, that is not a failure. It's a miss. And if you as the leader put those unrealistic expectations on them, then the failure was yours, not theirs. Admit you were wrong, apologize to the team, and let them know it wasn't their fault.

3. WHAT SUCCESSES CAN WE FIND IN THE FAILURE?

There's an old saying: "The gem cannot be polished without friction, nor man perfected without trials." No matter what kind of failure a team experiences, there is always a potential jewel of success contained in it. Sometimes it may be difficult to find. But your team members can discover it if they're willing to look for it.

My friend Warren Wiersbe used to say, "A realist is an idealist who has gone through the fire and been purified. A skeptic is an idealist who has gone through the fire and been burned." Don't allow the fire of adversity to make you a skeptic. Allow it to purify you.

WHETHER WE PUT UNREALISTIC EXPECTATION ON OURSELVES OR SOMEONE ELSE DID, IF A GOAL IS UNREALISTIC AND THE TEAM MISSES IT, THAT IS NOT A FAILURE. IT'S A MISS.

---

4. WHAT CAN WE LEARN FROM WHAT HAPPENED?

I enjoyed reading the comic strip *Peanuts* by Charles Schulz. One of my favorites has Charlie Brown at the beach building a beautiful sandcastle. As he stands back to admire his work, it is suddenly consumed by a huge wave. Looking at the smooth sand mound that had been his creation a moment before, he says, "There must be a lesson here, but I don't know what it is."

That's the way many people approach adversity. They

are so consumed by the events they experience that they become bewildered and miss the whole learning experience. But there is always a way to learn from failures and mistakes. Poet Lord Byron was right when he stated, "Adversity is the first path to truth."

"A REALIST IS AN IDEALIST WHO HAS GONE THROUGH THE FIRE AND BEEN PURIFIED."

—WARREN WIERSBE

It's difficult to give general guidelines about how to learn from mistakes, because every situation is different. But if you maintain a teachable attitude and coach your team members to do the same, you can find the lesson in any loss. Look for *anything* the group could do differently in the future to improve results.

5. ARE WE GRATEFUL FOR THE EXPERIENCE?

One of the ways to maintain a teachable mindset is to cultivate an attitude of gratitude. And that's possible even in the face of great disappointment.

"ADVERSITY IS THE FIRST PATH TO TRUTH."—LORD BYRON

For example, American sprinter Eddie Hart missed a preliminary heat for the 100-meter sprint in the 1972 Olympics in Munich. As a result, he lost his chance to win an individual gold medal. But his perspective on the experience was good. He said, "Everything you pursue you won't always attain. That's probably the most important lesson I learned from missing that race. There are times in life when you may not get the raise you want, the job you want. You have to learn to live with your defeats. And athletics are valuable, because they're all about winning and losing. Before you can actually be a good winner, you have to know how to lose."

Hart was grateful for the medal he received as a member of the relay team—and for the lesson it taught him about living with defeats. Encourage your team members to do the same. Cultivating a sense of gratitude in the face of adversity is one of the most important steps people can take to develop resilience.

6. HOW CAN WE TURN THIS INTO A SUCCESS?

Author William Marston says, "If there is any single factor that makes for success in living, it is the ability to draw dividends from defeat. Every success I know has been reached because the person was able to analyze defeat and actually profit from it in the next undertaking."

Determining what went wrong in a situation has value. But taking that analysis another step and figuring out how to use it to your benefit is a real difference-maker. Sometimes the benefit comes from learning something that will help you avoid similar mistakes in the future. Other times it is a serendipitous discovery, such as Edison's phonograph or Schönbein's smokeless gunpowder. If you're willing to try, you can often salvage something of value from any disaster.

"EVERY SUCCESS I KNOW HAS BEEN REACHED BECAUSE THE PERSON WAS ABLE TO ANALYZE DEFEAT AND ACTUALLY PROFIT FROM IT IN THE NEXT UNDERTAKING."—WILLIAM MARSTON

---

7. WHO CAN HELP US WITH THIS ISSUE?

People say there are two kinds of learning: experience, which is gained from your own mistakes, and wisdom, which is learned from the mistakes of others. I recommend that you teach your team to learn from the mistakes of others as much as possible.

Learning from failures is always easier when you get the help of wise counselors. There are many people in my life whom I've asked for advice after making huge blunders: my dad, Jack Hayford, Elmer Towns, and of course my wife, Margaret (who is always willing to share her perspective of my blunders with me).

Of course, who you choose to listen to matters. I heard a story about a newly appointed public servant who was setting himself up in his new office. As he sat at his desk for the first time, he discovered that his predecessor had left him three envelopes with advice with instructions that each be opened only in a time of great distress.

Before long, the public servant was in trouble with the press, so he decided to open envelope number one. It said, "Blame your predecessor." So that's what he did.

For a while things went smoothly. But a few months later, he was in trouble again, so he opened the second envelope. It said, "Reorganize." So that's what he did.

That bought him some more time. But because he had never really resolved any of the issues that were causing him problems, he ended up in trouble again, and this time it was even greater than before. In desperation, he opened the last envelope.

The note inside simply said, "Prepare three envelopes."

Whose advice would your team benefit from

receiving? Make sure it's someone who has *successfully* handled their challenges.

8. WHERE DO I GO FROM HERE?

Finally, once all the thinking is done, your team will need to take action putting into place what they've learned. In their book *Everyone's a Coach,* Don Shula and Ken Blanchard state, "Learning is defined as a change in behavior. You haven't learned a thing until you can take action and use it."[1]

"YOU HAVEN'T LEARNED A THING UNTIL YOU CAN TAKE ACTION AND USE IT."—SHULA AND BLANCHARD

When you are able to learn from any bad experience and thereby turn it into a good experience, you make a major transition in life. If you can teach your team members how to do that, it's a major transition for them and your organization. Many teams are kept so busy doing and working in an attempt to achieve goals that they never slow down, examine what isn't working, and improve. And that's a shame.

Business author Jim Zabloski says, "Contrary to popular belief, I consider failure a necessity in business. If you're not failing at least five times a day, you're probably not doing enough. The more you do, the more you fail. The more you fail, the more you learn. The more you learn, the better you get. The operative word here is *learn*. If you repeat the same mistake two or three times, you are not learning from it. You must learn from your own mistakes and from the mistakes of others before you."[2]

That ability to learn from mistakes and take advantage of adversity has value not just in business but in all aspects of life. But you must take the time to go through the process to receive the value of it.

CHAPTER 8

COACH TEAM MEMBERS TO OVERCOME THEIR FEARS

Fear is one of the greatest thieves of potential. And one of the greatest gifts you can give your team is the ability to overcome their fears, take on new challenges, and accomplish their dreams.

Psychologist Randall B. Hamrock observed, "In twenty years [of practice as a psychologist] I've talked with, tested, and given vocational counsel to at least 10,000 young men and women. One characteristic that almost all had was the tendency to sell themselves short." Fear robs us of our potential. It makes us smaller than we really are. One of the greatest mistakes we can make in life is to be in constant fear that we will make mistakes.

Tony Award–winning actor René Auberjonois stated, "Show me a guy who's afraid to look bad and I'll show you a guy you can beat every time." Why would he say that? Because when we give in to fear, we are already beaten. People who are ruled by fear stay where it's safe. And that's sad because people can't reach their potential by staying where it's safe. Worse yet, they keep others from reaching their potential too. When a leader is ruled by fear, he becomes a lid to the people who follow him. But when leaders break through their fears and help their team members do the same, their team can become unstoppable.

"SHOW ME A GUY WHO'S AFRAID
TO LOOK BAD AND I'LL SHOW YOU A GUY
YOU CAN BEAT EVERY TIME."
—RENÉ AUBERJONOIS

FEAR IS NATURAL

Fear is a normal part of human nature, and it always has been. Trace through human history, and you can find plenty of quotes on fear. Here are a few:

- Lucretius (ca. 60 BC)—"For as children tremble and fear everything in the blind darkness, so we in the light sometimes fear what is no more to be feared than the things children in the dark hold in terror and imagine will come true."
- Michel Eyquem de Montaigne (1580)—"The thing I fear most is fear."

- Francis Bacon (1623)—"Nothing is terrible except fear itself."
- Duke of Wellington (1831)—"The only thing I am afraid of is fear."

But just because it's normal doesn't mean we should give in to it.

An old German adage says, "Fear makes the wolf bigger than he is." An interesting illustration of this from U.S. history occurred during the American Revolution. The story goes that after the Bahamas were captured by Spain, Andrew Deveaux, a lieutenant colonel of South Carolina, recruited a handful of militiamen and Harbour Island settlers because he planned to take Nassau back using a clever strategy.

In April of 1783 with only two hundred men, Deveaux managed to capture the high ground on the island after a brief skirmish, even though the Spanish had a much larger force. The Spaniards then watched as Deveaux repeatedly ferried load after load of men from his ships to his defensive position onshore. But what the Spaniards didn't know was that the same men kept going back and forth, standing on their trip over to the island and hiding themselves by laying down in the boat on the trip back to the ships. The leader of the Spanish troops believed he was outnumbered, and his fear got the better of him. Believing he would be defeated at the hands of a large force in a defensible position, he surrendered.

"FEAR MAKES THE WOLF BIGGER THAN HE IS."
—OLD GERMAN ADAGE

William Shakespeare's play *Measure for Measure* includes these lines:

> Our doubts are traitors
> and make us lose the good we oft might win
> by fearing to attempt."

That was certainly true in this incident from history.

HOW TO HELP TEAM MEMBERS HANDLE FEAR

If your team members have been too tentative and lack confidence, you will need to coach them to handle fear instead of getting handled by it. I believe fear can be overcome by anyone if they get the right help. Here are the steps I recommend you take with them.

1. ASK THEM TO ADMIT THEIR FEARS

Nobody can overcome their fears unless they first recognize that they exist. Ask team members to make a list of what makes them feel fear. If they seem unable to sit down and do that, it may be that they are unwilling to deal with those feelings. If that is the case, ask them to start by trying to tune in to what they're feeling. When does their heart race for no apparent reason? When do they feel paralyzed by inaction? When do they display nervous energy for no apparent reason? These kinds of responses may be due to fear.

2. HELP THEM DISCOVER THE SOURCE OF THEIR FEAR

A man who had a morbid fear of thunder went to see a noted psychiatrist for treatment.

"You have a condition called brontophobia," the doctor said to the man. "It's silly to be afraid of thunder at your age. Just think of it as a drum roll in the symphony of life."

"What if that doesn't work?" the man asked.

"Well, then do as I do. When you hear thunder, stuff cotton in your ears, crawl under the bed, and sing 'Mary Had a Little Lamb' at the top of your voice until it stops."

Most people's fears are based not on facts but on feelings. I think of *fear* as False Expectations Appearing Real. You have to look beyond the irrational feelings you may possess and discover the expectations that lie beneath them. American humorist James Thurber wrote, "All men should strive to learn before they die what they are running from and to and why." That is the next step in the process.

3. SHOW THEM HOW THEIR FEARS ARE LIMITING THEM

Philosopher and Catholic cardinal J. H. Newman advised, "Fear not that your life will come to an end but that it will never have a beginning." That's what can happen if you let fear take over your life. Honestly, most of our fears are totally unfounded. In fact, studies have shown that 95 percent of what we fear is baseless.[1] The rest are simply things we must learn to live with. Maybe the best approach is to adopt the attitude of poet Gertrude Stein, who said, "Considering how dangerous everything is, nothing is really frightening."

"ALL MEN SHOULD STRIVE TO LEARN BEFORE THEY DIE WHAT THEY ARE RUNNING FROM AND TO AND WHY."—JAMES THURBER

Remind your team members that there are no guarantees in life. People look for many things to protect them: burglar alarms, traveler's checks, aspirin, umbrellas, GPS systems, and air bags. But the truth is that life is dangerous, damaging to our health, and will eventually kill us. So we might as well live life to the fullest.

STUDIES SHOW THAT 95 PERCENT OF WHAT WE FEAR IS BASELESS.

4. HELP THEM SEE FEAR AS THE NORMAL PRICE OF PROGRESS

One of the secrets of success is not letting what you cannot do interfere with what you can do. Millionaire entrepreneur and philanthropist W. Clement Stone started his business career at age five selling newspapers and was selling insurance full time at age sixteen. He never let fear stop him from being successful. A strong proponent of positive thinking, Stone said that the secret to making sales was going where you do not want to go and doing what you do not want to do. That's often what you and your team members need to be willing to do to be successful.

ONE OF THE SECRETS OF SUCCESS IS NOT LETTING WHAT YOU CANNOT DO INTERFERE WITH WHAT YOU CAN DO.

I've found this to be true in my own career. Today I am known most for my public speaking. But when I first started speaking, I wasn't effective. I remember how fearful I was when I got started. The first time I got to speak at an event as a senior in college, I was terrible. People who knew me then described my speaking style as "stiff." But despite my fear and shortcomings, I kept at it. I began to study effective communicators and spoke to small audiences at every opportunity. It took me seven years to overcome my fear and discomfort while speaking. Only then could I develop and hone my communication style.

Over the years, I've spoken to audiences more than ten thousand times. I've spoken to small audiences and ones that filled a stadium. But when I was afraid during those early speaking engagements, I had no idea where it would lead me. If I had allowed my fear to rule me, I never would have gotten anywhere. Instead, I accepted fear as the price I would have to pay for personal progress and eventual success. You need to help the members of your team understand that they must also pay a price to reach their potential. There's an age-old proverb saying this: He is not worthy of the honeycomb who shuns the hive because the bees have stingers.

5. CONVERT THEIR FEAR INTO DESIRE

Boxing trainer and manager Cus D'Amato stated, "The hero and the coward both feel the same thing, but the hero uses his fear, projects it onto his opponent, while the coward runs. It's the same thing, fear, but it's what you do with it that matters."[2] Just about every negative emotion we feel can be converted into something positive to help us get further in life.

Afraid of poverty? Convert it to a positive work ethic.
Afraid of greediness? Convert it to generosity.
Afraid of rejection? Convert it to an ability to connect with people.
Afraid of insignificance? Convert it to the service of others.

HE IS NOT WORTHY OF THE HONEYCOMB WHO SHUNS THE HIVE BECAUSE THE BEES HAVE STINGERS.

What are some ways you can coach your team members to convert their fears into desires? How can they embrace the adaptability that comes with greater resilience? How can they follow the advice of Roger Babson, founder of Babson College and Webber International University, who remarked, "If things go wrong, don't go with them." Show them a new way. They can turn their lives around by taking the very thing that once created fear in them, and using the energy it created to do something positive and worthwhile.

6. FOCUS THEM ON THINGS THEY CAN CONTROL

There are many things in this life that we cannot control. There's no good reason to worry about those things. Writer Harold Stephens observed, "There is a great difference between worry and concern. A worried person sees a problem, and a concerned person solves a problem."

What are the things your people can control? The first is their attitude. Often, we wish we could control other people's actions to make life easier for ourselves. But we know that's not possible. Instead, we need to control our attitude toward others when we're not happy with our interactions with them. Remember, what happens *to* you isn't as important as what happens *in* you.

"IF THINGS GO WRONG, DON'T GO WITH THEM."—ROGER BABSON

The second thing we can control is our calendar. We may not be able to control today's circumstances, but we can do our best to plan the time we have. Most people who fear the future do so because they don't prepare for it. Teach your team members these two truths, and you will not only help them lessen their fears; you will also help them develop resilience.

7. EMPHASIZE TODAY—NOT YESTERDAY OR TOMORROW

Yesterday and tomorrow seem to clamor for our attention. Yesterday wants us to second-guess past decisions and fret over whether we did the right thing. As President Harry Truman said, "If you've done the best you can—if you have done what you have to do—there is no use worrying about it, because nothing can change it." Tomorrow wants us to focus on what *might* happen. But focusing on the future can cause us to miss present opportunities. I love what former first lady Barbara Bush said about the future, comparing it to a train ride:

> We get on board that train at birth, and we want to cross the continent because we have in mind that somewhere out there is a station. We pass by sleepy little towns looking out the window of life's train, grain fields and silos, level grade crossings, buses full of people on the roads beside us. We pass by cities and factories, but we don't look at any of it because we want to get to the station. We believe that out there is a station where a band is playing and banners are hung and flags are waving, and when we get there that will be life's destination. We don't really get to know anybody on the train. We pace up and down the aisles looking at our watches eager to get to the station because we know that life has a station for us.

> This station changes for us during life. To begin with, for most of us, it's turning 18, getting out of high school. Then the station is that first promotion and then the station becomes getting the kids out of college, and then the station becomes retirement and then . . . all too late we recognize the truth—that this side of that city whose builder is God, there really isn't a station. The joy is in the journey and the journey is the joy.
>
> Sooner or later, you realize there is no station and the truth of life is the trip. Read a book, eat more ice cream, go barefoot more often, hug a child, go fishing, laugh more. The station will come soon enough. And as you go, find a way to make this world more beautiful.[3]

Most people arrive at a different destination than they expect in life—some better, some worse, but all different. So focusing on the destination is not a good idea. Besides, tomorrow may come; it may not. There are no guarantees. So focusing too much on yesterday or tomorrow just wastes our energy.

The only place we really have any power is in the present. We don't want to be like the character in the "Ziggy" cartoon who laments, "The present is what slips by us while we're pondering the past and worrying about the future," or like writer Mark Twain, who joked, "I've been through some terrible things in my life, a few of which actually happened." Teach your team members to do what they can in the here and now—despite their fear—and they will have the satisfaction of knowing that they are doing everything within their power to reach their potential.

8. FEED THE RIGHT EMOTION AND STARVE THE WRONG ONE

In life, both faith and fear will arise within you, and you choose which one will prevail. Someone once wrote,

> Two natures beat within my breast,
> The one is foul, the other blessed.
> The one I love, the other I hate;
> The one I feed will dominate.[4]

The thing is, both of those emotions will *always* be present in us. The emotion we continually feed is the one that will dominate our lives. We can't expect fear to simply disappear. If we continually focus on our fears, entertain them, and give in to them, they will increase. The way to ultimately overcome them is to starve them.

"I'VE BEEN THROUGH SOME TERRIBLE THINGS IN MY LIFE, A FEW OF WHICH ACTUALLY HAPPENED."—MARK TWAIN

Teach your people not to give their fears any of their time or energy. Encourage them not to feed them with gossip or negative news shows or frightening movies. Instead, ask them to focus on and feed their faith, their belief in themselves and others. The more energy and time they give to their faith, the stronger it will become. And coach them in this: Anytime they feel afraid of doing something but go ahead and do it anyway, they will be reprogramming themselves for success and developing their resilience. When they feel fear, it means "go" instead of "stop," and "fight harder" instead of "give up."

Former first lady Eleanor Roosevelt once wrote, "You gain strength, courage and confidence by every experience in which you really stop to look fear in the face. You are able to say to yourself, 'I lived through this horror. I can take the next thing that comes along.' You must do the thing you think you cannot do."

That is what overcoming fear may be to you and your team—doing what you think you can't. If you let fear stop you, then you will go from "I think I can't" to "I can't because I didn't." But if you face your fears and move forward, you give you and your team the best shot at success, and you build resilience that will come to your aid the next time you face adversity.

CHAPTER 9

CHAMPION CHANGE AS NECESSARY FOR SUCCESS

On August 3, 1492, Columbus set sail from Palos in southern Spain in search of a western route to Asia. He was convinced that the world was round, despite the belief by nearly everyone else in Europe that it was flat. Most people believed that a ship sailing due west would fall off the edge of the earth!

Columbus didn't find the route he sought, but he did confirm his suspicions that the earth was a sphere. And after months of exploration and the loss of one ship, he returned to Palos on March 15, 1493—a hero. And in a matter of months, the perspective of everyone in Europe concerning the earth changed drastically. It caused a quick and transforming revolution of the world. Right? Not exactly.

Columbus was considered a hero for returning from his venture. And he was credited with discovering new lands. But people didn't change their minds about the earth. As David Bayles and Ted Orland, authors of *Art and Fear,* state, when Columbus returned from the New World and proclaimed the earth was round, almost everyone else went right on believing the earth was flat. Then they died. The *next* generation grew up believing the world was round. That's how people change their minds.[1]

Does it seem to you that your team is as willing to change as the people in Columbus's time? If so, that's not surprising. Everyone resists change. For many years I thought leaders liked change and everyone else didn't. As a visionary leader, I always felt that I was drawing reluctant team members into the future. But I finally realized that leaders don't like change any more than followers do—unless, of course, it's their idea!

WHY PEOPLE RESIST CHANGE

Change is hard for everyone. Novelist Mark Twain said, "The only person who likes change is a wet baby." Truly, change is one of the greatest attitude obstacles your team will ever face. Why? There are many reasons:

PEOPLE FEAR PERSONAL LOSS

Whenever change is imminent, the first question that pops into people's minds is how the change will affect them. For example, imagine that a coworker came up to you today and said, "I just heard that the boss is laying off some people today." Was your first thought, *I wonder what market conditions precipitated such a decision?* Or was it, *Boy, I bet the boss feels bad about having to do that?* Or, *I wonder how that will impact the bottom line of the company?* No, chances are your first thought was, *Am I at risk?* That's just human nature.

In the moments that we face change, we can suddenly feel vulnerable.

"THE ONLY PERSON WHO LIKES CHANGE IS A WET BABY."—MARK TWAIN

Optimistic people will more quickly see some good in most changes, but the truth is that there is loss even in positive changes. Ralph Waldo Emerson said, "For everything you gain, you lose something." In life there are wins and losses. Even when change is good, we are sometimes forced to give up things that are important to us.

Back in 1996 when I decided to relocate my companies from San Diego to Atlanta, it was the right move for many reasons, and it was a win for the organization. However, it meant leaving many good friends, a place that felt like home, and the best weather in the world. It was a win that contained losses. As poet and literary critic

Paul Valéry observed, "Every beginning is a consequence. Every beginning ends something."

When you need to lead your team or organization through change, be aware that your people will be afraid of losses, and some of their fears will be legitimate. If you're sensitive to this and are willing to acknowledge their fears, it will go a long way toward helping them.

> "EVERY BEGINNING IS A CONSEQUENCE. EVERY BEGINNING ENDS SOMETHING."—PAUL VALÉRY

THEY FEAR THE UNKNOWN

I love a story that my friend Zig Ziglar used to tell: A man from out in the sticks won a bass fiddle in a drawing. He took it home and looked at the beginning music book that came with it. Unfortunately, the book had been damaged and the only part that survived intact was one page showing the left hand in one position on the strings and the right hand drawing the bow. So he carefully placed his fingers and drew the bow back and forth across the strings, producing an awful sound. And though it was the only sound he could make, he practiced every day. This of course drove his wife crazy.

Then one day his wife went to a concert, and by chance her seat was not very far from the bass fiddle player in the orchestra. She was delighted by the sound this player produced with his instrument, and she watched as his fingers traveled up and down the instrument's fret board and the bow moved in various rhythms. It was beautiful.

As she traveled home, she decided that she wanted to communicate to old Johnny One Note the potential of his instrument, but she also knew that he was easily upset. As it happened, the man was practicing when she arrived at home.

"Honey," she said, "may I ask you a question?"

"Sure," he answered, continuing to saw at the strings.

"At the concert I noticed that the bass fiddle player kept moving his left hand up and down and left and right while his right hand moved slowly on some occasions and fast on others." She said this gently, not wanting to upset him. "I'm just curious why he moves his hands so much and does so many things while you keep your hands in exactly the same spot all the time."

"That's easy," he answered. "That old boy's still lookin' for his place, and I done found mine!"

People often avoid change because they worry about the unknown. People often cling to what they know, even if they are not satisfied with it. Fear holds them back. As a leader, you can answer some of the questions to reduce the number of unknowns they have to face. And you can coach them to be ready for the unknowns that will surface over time.

THEY WORRY THE TIMING IS WRONG

Law 19 in my book *The 21 Irrefutable Laws of Leadership* states, "When to lead is as important as what to do and where to go." What happens when you try to make a change at the wrong time? For that matter, when is the right time to make changes? From a leadership point of view, there are better times for change than others. I developed the following checklist to help me navigate the process:

- Will this change benefit the followers?
- Is this change compatible with the purpose of the organization?
- Is this change specific and clear?
- Are the top 20 percent (the influencers) in favor of this change?
- Is it possible to test this change before making a total commitment to it?
- Are physical, financial, and human resources available to make this change?
- Is this change reversible?
- Is this change the next obvious step?
- Does this change have both short- and long-range benefits?
- Is the leadership of the team or organization capable of bringing about this change?
- Does everything else indicate the timing is right?

Before implementing a big change, I run through this checklist and answer each question with a yes or no. If too many questions have a no by them, then I know I might need to rethink it because the timing may not be right.

THEY KNOW CHANGE FEELS AWKWARD

When was the last time you did something for the first time? Can you name something specific? It must be something really new. Seeing a new movie doesn't count—because you've seen a movie before. It needs to be a real first. If you can't remember, then you might be in trouble.

WHEN WAS THE LAST TIME YOU DID SOMETHING FOR THE FIRST TIME?

I want you to do an experiment. Don't get annoyed by it; just trust me. First, I want you to get ready to set this book down and clasp your hands together, palms together with your fingers interlocked. Try it.

If I asked you to do this process ten times—which I won't—you would lock your fingers together the same way every time, with one particular thumb over the other.

Now I want you to try something. Put the book down again and clasp your hands together again, but this time I want you to interlock your fingers in such a way that the other thumb is on top. Try it.

Didn't that feel weird? That's what change does—it makes you feel awkward. It isn't wrong; it's just different, and that takes us out of our comfort zone. As a leader, if you reassure your team members that they will feel uncomfortable during change and that it's normal, it will help them trust the process.

THEY CLING TO TRADITION

Cambridge University professor F. M. Cornford quipped, "Nothing is ever done until everyone is convinced that it ought to be done and has been convinced for so long that it is now time to do something else." Many people cling to tradition. The assumption is that if something is tradition, it must be the best way. But that's not necessarily so. Here's a riddle that shows what I mean: How many traditionalists does it take to change a light bulb? The answer is four: one to change it and three to talk about how wonderful the old bulb was.

If a tradition connects you to other people or to your personal history, it can be a good thing. If it doesn't, then it may be time to try something else. Good leaders help their team members to become more resilient by showing them why remaining the same is a poor choice and making a change is a better one.

PREPARATION POINTS FOR SUCCESSFUL CHANGE

Now that we've discussed the negative reasons people resist change, it's time to focus on some positive reasons.

1. POINT OUT CHANGE IS ALWAYS NECESSARY FOR IMPROVEMENT

I am not a proponent of change for its own sake. That's often a characteristic of restlessness and can be a symptom of personal inner conflict. Honestly, change can represent both possible opportunities and potential losses. Even though all progress brings change, not all change brings progress. But as leadership expert Max

De Pree observed, "We cannot become what we need by remaining what we are." If you desire growth, then you must embrace change.

"WE CANNOT BECOME WHAT WE NEED BY REMAINING WHAT WE ARE."—MAX DE PREE

General Douglas MacArthur stated, "Life is a lively process of becoming. If you haven't added to your interests within the past year, if you are thinking the same old thoughts, relating the same personal experiences, having the same predictable reactions, rigor mortis of the personality has set in."

If the people you're leading want a better future, help them understand that if they don't change the direction they are going, they will never get it. When we want something we've never had, then we must do something we've never done. That means changing.

2. ENCOURAGE THEM TO ACCEPT THAT CHANGE WILL HAPPEN ANYWAY

A British duke once said, "Any change at any time for any reason is to be deplored." I feel sorry for people like him. They have a hard time dealing with reality and as a result, they experience a difficult life. Change is unavoidable. The only thing certain about tomorrow is that it will be different from today. If you doubt that, consider this: My grandfather had a farm, my parents had a garden, and I've got a can opener! It's a different world than it was twenty years ago, and it will be different in another twenty. Encourage your team to accept and maybe even embrace what they cannot avoid.

IF THE PEOPLE YOU'RE LEADING WANT A BETTER FUTURE, HELP THEM UNDERSTAND THAT IF THEY DON'T CHANGE THE DIRECTION THEY ARE GOING, THEY WILL NEVER GET IT.

3. BE TRANSPARENT ABOUT THE PRICE OF CHANGE

American dramatist and screenwriter Sidney Howard remarked, "One-half of knowing what you want is knowing what you must give up before you get it." Change always costs you something, if not in money, then in time, energy, and creativity. In fact, if change doesn't cost you anything, then it might not be real change.

> "ONE-HALF OF KNOWING WHAT YOU WANT IS KNOWING WHAT YOU MUST GIVE UP BEFORE YOU GET IT."—SIDNEY HOWARD

As you consider how to help your team make the changes needed to improve and grow, it is important to measure the cost of change compared to the cost of the status quo and communicate it to the members of your team. You will need to do your homework. That often makes the difference between *Growth = Change* and *Change = Grief*.

What will the changes your team needs to make really cost?

Management expert Tom Peters gave his perspective on this. He said, "Don't rock the boat. Sink it and start over." If you desire to be creative and do something highly innovative, that's sometimes what it takes. You must destroy the old to create something new. But you must prepare your team to deal with something so drastic and dramatic. Otherwise, you may end up sinking yourself as a leader.

4. SHOW THEM CHANGE HAPPENS FROM THE INSIDE OUT

I love the *Peanuts* comic strip by Charles Schulz in which Lucy says to Charlie Brown, "I would like to change the world."

"Where would you start?" Charlie Brown asks her.

Lucy's simple reply: "I would start with you."

I hate to say it, but our attitude is probably a lot more

like Lucy's than we would care to admit. If we don't like something, we desire change—for everyone other than us!

Novelist Frances Hodgson Burnett wrote,

> At first people refuse to believe that a strange
> new thing can be done,
> and then they begin to hope it can be done,
> then they see it can be done—
> then it is done and all the world wonders why
> it was not done centuries ago.[2]

"DON'T ROCK THE BOAT. SINK IT AND START OVER."—TOM PETERS

Artist Andy Warhol observed, "They always say that time changes things, but you actually have to change them yourself." The truth is that any change that occurs in the world always begins first with change within an individual. That's why playwright George Bernard Shaw said, "Progress is impossible without change; and those who cannot change their minds cannot change anything."

"PROGRESS IS IMPOSSIBLE WITHOUT CHANGE; AND THOSE WHO CANNOT CHANGE THEIR MINDS CANNOT CHANGE ANYTHING."—GEORGE BERNARD SHAW

As a leader, you must assist your team members in accepting change internally so that you can create change organizationally. If you can get them to dedicate themselves to growth and teach them to develop a lifestyle of planned improvement, change begins to feel more normal to them. And personal development becomes their expectation.

It is said that pianist Arthur Rubinstein refused to

listen to recordings made of songs he had played. Even only a few months after he had completed them, he was dissatisfied with the playing he heard. Why? Because he had grown and changed, but the recordings had not.

5. DON'T ASK THEM TO CHANGE THEIR CONVICTIONS

I have to admit that I'm a personal growth fanatic. There are few things I enjoy more than learning something new. My father got me started when I was a kid. He paid me to read books that would help me learn and grow. Now I'm in my late seventies, and I still love it when I can see myself improving in an area I've targeted for growth. But as much as I am dedicated to progress, there are some things that I'm not willing to change—no matter what—such as my faith and my values. I'd rather die than forfeit my faith in God or my commitment to integrity, family, generosity, and belief in people. Some things are not worth compromising at any price.

I want to encourage you to think about the nonnegotiables in your life. What are you willing to live and die for? Write down the things you will hold on to no matter what, and take some time to explain why. Once you've done this yourself, encourage your team members to do the same. This is important for them to maintain their integrity. But it also creates perspective. Let them know you will never ask them to violate their principles. But for everything else, they should be open to change.

6. COMMUNICATE THAT IT'S NEVER TOO LATE TO CHANGE

I already mentioned that I am in my late seventies. The older I get, the more I meet people my age who express regret for the way they've lived their lives. Sometimes the regret is for things they've done, but more often it is for things they didn't do but felt that they should have tried. If they ask for my advice, I quote one of my favorite sayings:

> Though you cannot go back
> And make a brand-new start, my friend.
> Anyone can start from now
> And make a brand-new end.

It's never too late to change. As the Turkish proverb

says, "No matter how far you have gone on a wrong road, turn back." Let your team know that altering their course and accepting change isn't a sign of weakness. It's a sign of strength. Encourage them to do it.

Nearly every organization sets improvement as one of its most important goals. Today we hear many leaders talk about small, incremental improvements: "Try to get 1 percent better every day." Inherent in that idea is the inevitable process of change. For that reason, you need to continually help the people on your team to expect change, want change, embrace change, and champion change. If they're willing to start that journey, they will become more resilient. And they will grow, the team will improve, and everyone will be in a better position for success.

"NO MATTER HOW FAR YOU HAVE GONE ON A WRONG ROAD, TURN BACK."—TURKISH PROVERB

CHAPTER 10

TEACH TEAM MEMBERS TO BECOME PROBLEM SOLVERS

One day I was flipping through a magazine when an A.D. for a company called Accenture caught my eye. The page showed golfer Tiger Woods on a golf green leaning down to line up a putt. He was holding his putter in his left hand, and he had just set down his ball. His gaze was highly focused—burningly intense—on the hole. At the top of the page were the words "Waiting for ideal conditions is rarely an option." Only after reading those words did I realize that in the foreground of the picture was a man in heavy rain gear squeegeeing a lot of water off the green in preparation for the putt. Evidently, Woods was plying his craft in the midst of a downpour, yet it wasn't fazing him a bit. Right below the image of Woods it says, "Go on. Be a Tiger."

LEADERS AND THEIR PROBLEMS

That's the way life works much of the time, isn't it? We try to get things done—whether work, play, family time, or something else—and we find ourselves having to do so in the midst of storms. And if you're a leader, you may feel that acutely. If you're leading a team during a difficult season or working in an organization that lacks momentum, you may feel that you have nothing *but* problems.

However, resilient leaders see problems as opportunities. Why? Because leaders capable of solving problems are coveted in organizations. They help move the organization forward and they rise more quickly than other leaders. And if they have the capacity to develop teams that also solve problems, their value is even higher.

Here are the differences between people with right and wrong perspectives on problems:

A WRONG PERSPECTIVE	A RIGHT PERSPECTIVE
Problems are unsolvable.	Problems are solvable.
Problems are permanent.	Problems are temporary.
Problems are not normal.	Problems are a normal part of life.
Problems make us bitter.	Problems make us better.
Problems control us.	Problems challenge us.
Problems stop us.	Problems stretch us.

As a result of their correct perspective, here are some of the characteristics that set them apart from other leaders.

1. GOOD LEADERS ANTICIPATE PROBLEMS

Al Davis, the late owner of the NFL's Oakland Raiders, said, "A great leader doesn't treat problems as special. He treats them as normal." If you're working, expect problems. If you're dealing with family, expect problems. If you're just minding your own business and trying to relax, expect problems. If everything goes according to plan, then be pleasantly surprised. If it doesn't and you've planned accordingly, then you won't get so frustrated. A problem not anticipated is a problem. A problem anticipated is an opportunity. Good leaders know this, and it makes them more resilient.

RESILIENT LEADERS SEE PROBLEMS AS OPPORTUNITIES.

2. GOOD LEADERS EMBRACE EACH PROBLEM AS A POTENTIAL OPPORTUNITY

President John F. Kennedy was once asked how he became a war hero. His response: "It was quite easy. Somebody sunk my boat!" While it is true that certain individuals have a vision for innovation or change and they pursue it with purpose, the majority of the time adversity paves our way for success. That was the case for King

Gillette, who was so tired of sharpening his straight razor that he developed the safety razor with disposable blades. It was true for Chester Greenwood, who suffered from frostbitten ears and consequently developed earmuffs. It was true for Humphrey O'Sullivan, a printer, who grew tired of coworkers stealing the rubber mat he stood on to work and created rubber heels for his shoes. And it was the case for a man whose small shop was in tough straits financially. He recalled,

> I was paying a sheriff $5 a day to postpone a judgment on my small factory. Then came the gas man, and because I could not pay his bill promptly, he cut off my gas. I was in the midst of certain very important experiments, and to have the gas people plunge me into darkness made me so mad that I at once began to read up on gas technique and economics, and resolved I would try to see if electricity couldn't be made to replace gas and give those gas people a run for their money.[1]

That man was Thomas Edison, founder of the Edison General Electric Company, which later became General Electric.

Problems are wake-up calls for creativity. If we use problems to open our eyes, our problems will prompt us and our teams to use our abilities, rally our resources, and move us forward.

PROBLEMS ARE WAKE-UP CALLS FOR CREATIVITY.

3. ASK TEAM MEMBERS TO BECOME PROBLEMS SOLVERS, NOT PROBLEM SPOTTERS

Cartoonist Ashleigh Brilliant remarked, "I don't have any solutions, but I certainly admire the problem." Isn't that the way some people operate? They're very quick to find any kind of problem and point it out. We don't want the members of our teams to be problem *spotters*. We want to teach them to become problem *solvers*.

Problems are easy to see. Some people even see problems that don't exist! Look at these reported remarks taken from registration sheets and comment cards returned to the staff at the Bridger Wilderness Area in Wyoming:

- Trails need to be wider so people can walk holding hands.
- Trails need to be reconstructed. Please avoid building trails that go uphill.
- Too many bugs and leeches and spiders and spiderwebs. Please spray the wilderness to rid the area of these pests.
- Please pave the trails so they can be plowed of snow during the winter.
- Chairlifts need to be in some places so that we can get to wonderful views without having to hike to them.
- The coyotes made too much noise last night and kept me awake. Please eradicate these annoying animals.
- A small deer came into my camp and stole my jar of pickles. Is there a way I can get reimbursed?
- Reflectors need to be placed on trees every 50 feet so people can hike at night with flashlights.

- Escalators would help on steep hill sections.
- A McDonald's would be nice at the trailhead.
- The places where trails do not exist are not well marked.
- Too many rocks in the mountains.[2]

There's a world of difference between a person who sees a problem and a person who solves a problem. It's said that legal immigrants in the United States are far more likely than native-born Americans to become millionaires. They do this despite the additional obstacles they often face, such as language differences, culture shock, separation from family, and isolation. Why? Because they are resilient problem solvers. That's what we need to teach our team members to become.

PROBLEM-SOLVING TEAMS

I want to help you understand how to teach the members of your team to become problems solvers. To do that, I'm going to start by making an assumption: They can see problems. And you've helped them to recognize problems for what they are—temporary tests of their resolve and ability. If you've been helping them to become more resilient, then they should be ready to start tackling problems themselves. Here is my advice on how they can do that:

1. FACE THE PROBLEM

Finding the solution to any problem you see starts with facing it. Many years ago, I saw a television commercial that depicted a family at home where the children were playing, the mother was vacuuming, and the father was reading the paper. They were meant to represent an average American family. But there was one problem. A huge elephant was in the room with them. Even though it was making everything they did difficult, and they were having to move around it, the family ignored the elephant and pretended it didn't exist. The A.D. was for alcoholism awareness. Difficult problems such as alcoholism create chaos in families, yet people often pretend that everything's fine. They can't address the problem, because they won't face the problem.

Author and former economic planner John Perkins

believed, "There are three kinds of people in our society: those who can't see or refuse to see the problems; those who see the problems and because they didn't personally create them are content to blame someone else; and those who see the problems and though they didn't create them are willing to assume personal responsibility for solving them." You want to help every member of your team to be people who assume responsibility and solve problems.

HELP EVERY MEMBER OF YOUR TEAM TO BE PEOPLE WHO ASSUME RESPONSIBILITY AND SOLVE PROBLEMS.

2. VERIFY THE PROBLEM AS A PROBLEM

Philosopher Abraham Kaplan made a useful distinction between problems and predicaments. He believed a problem was something you could do something about. If you can't do something about it, then it's not a problem. It's a predicament. That means it's something that must be coped with or endured, not solved.

IF YOU CAN'T DO SOMETHING ABOUT IT, THEN IT'S NOT A PROBLEM. IT'S A PREDICAMENT.

When people treat a predicament as a problem, they can become frustrated, angry, or depressed. They waste energy. They make bad decisions. And when people treat problems as predicaments, they often settle, give up, or see themselves as victims. And as a result, they fail to take action.

Let me give you a few examples to help you get a handle on what I mean. If you are married, chances are that if you are a morning person, your spouse is a night person (or vice versa). That is a predicament, not a problem. It's not something either of you can change. No one can expect another person to change the way they are wired internally. If you try to do that, you and your spouse will experience lots of conflict, and there will be no resolution. The problem then is how to deal with the difference. The difficulty you have for finding ways to spend time together because of your different wiring is something that can be solved.

Here is another example. Let's say you go to work one day and find out that the company you work for is out of business. It's done, and that means your job is gone. That is a predicament—unless you are in a position financially to buy the business. Assuming that you're not, then what are you going to do? Are you going to waste energy complaining about losing your job or trying to talk your boss into restarting the company? You'd be better off working on solving the problem of finding a new job or starting your own business. Resilient problem solvers often lose a job and use it as an opportunity to transition to something better. People who spend time and energy trying to solve a predicament just get frustrated. Help your team members to recognize the difference and act accordingly.

3. EVALUATE THE PROBLEM

It's been said that if you keep your head when all about you are losing theirs—then you don't understand the problem. Seriously though, if a serious problem doesn't cause you and your team to pause and take stock, then you probably haven't evaluated it properly. And that will create difficulties down the road, because if you've misjudged the size or scope of a problem, and when you have done that and try to deal with it anyway, you will inevitably come up against a wall, need to stop trying to solve it, reevaluate it, and start over again. That's why it's important to do an honest evaluation of trouble before you jump in with solutions.

Mike Leavitt, United States secretary of health and human services under President George W. Bush, said, "There is a time in the life of every problem when it is big enough to see, yet small enough to solve." The trick is to find the right timing and then to be patient when implementing the solution. Inexperienced people expect problems to be settled instantly. Experienced people are like the master sculptor who keeps striking at the chisel on the marble block with steady blows of the hammer.

Unlike the rookie who expects to split the stone with a single blow, the master knows that if he keeps working at it, he will eventually succeed.

"THERE IS A TIME IN THE LIFE OF EVERY PROBLEM WHEN IT IS BIG ENOUGH TO SEE, YET SMALL ENOUGH TO SOLVE."—MIKE LEAVITT

---

4. LIST ALL THE POTENTIAL WAYS TO SOLVE THE PROBLEM

Richard Wirthlin worked as President Ronald Reagan's pollster when he was in the White House. During those years, the president's approval rating varied widely. Right after the assassination attempt on Reagan's life, his rating was about 90 percent. A year later, in the midst of the recession of 1982, his numbers plummeted. Wirthlin recalls having to deliver those low figures to Reagan.

"Well, how was it? How are they? What do the figures look like?" the president asked.

"Well, they're pretty bad, Mr. President."

"How bad are they?"

"Well," answered Wirthlin, "they're about 32 percent."

"Dick, don't worry," said the president with a smile. "I'll just go out there and try to get shot again."[3]

Author and speaker Grenville Kleiser stated, "To every problem there is already a solution whether you know what it is or not." I would take that another step further. I believe every problem has many solutions. To find them, we need to fire up our creativity, apply sustained thinking, and pull together our resources. Included in those resources are people. The problems that surround us are not as crucial as the people around us.

THE PROBLEMS THAT SURROUND US ARE NOT AS CRUCIAL AS THE PEOPLE AROUND US.

One of my favorite activities is to pull together a group of good thinkers to solve a problem. We start by laying out the problem and talking about the potential impact. I usually prefer that someone in the group other than me take the lead because I want others engaged, thinking, and talking. Then we start brainstorming solutions. In these discussions, there is no rank, there are no titles, and seniority makes no difference. Everyone has a chance to generate ideas, and I encourage people to share ideas good, bad, and ugly. There's no such thing as a bad idea because even the worst idea can be the catalyst to the best idea. The idea is for the best ideas to win. And at the end of the day, our goal is to find a minimum of three good or great ideas.

5. DETERMINE THE BEST THREE WAYS TO SOLVE THE PROBLEM

What I love about brainstorming solutions is that the team comes up with many good options, and they learn to think and problem-solve from each other. After that, you can choose the solution that best serves the organization, but you also have other backup solutions ready and waiting.

You don't want to be like the older woman who was being tried for the murder of her third husband. The prosecuting lawyer asked, "What happened to your first husband?"

"He died of mushroom poisoning," said the woman.

"How about your second husband?"

"He died of mushroom poisoning too," she replied.

"Well then," the lawyer continued, "what about your third husband?"

"He died of a brain concussion."

"How did that happen?" asked the lawyer.

"He wouldn't eat the mushrooms."

Good thinkers always have more than one way to solve a problem. I believe people make mistakes when they think there is only one solution to any problem. You can't get fixated. You need to be resilient.

GOOD THINKERS ALWAYS HAVE MORE THAN ONE WAY TO SOLVE A PROBLEM.

6. IMPLEMENT THE SOLUTION WITH YOUR MISSION IN MIND

Ralph Waldo Emerson observed, "Concentration is the secret of strength in politics, in war, in trade, in short, in all management of human affairs." Where should you focus that concentration? On the mission. Always ask your team to implement solutions with the mission in mind.

"THE MEASURE OF SUCCESS IS NOT WHETHER YOU HAVE A TOUGH PROBLEM TO DEAL WITH, BUT WHETHER IT IS THE SAME PROBLEM YOU HAD LAST YEAR."—JOHN FOSTER DULLES

If the solution you chose turns out to be a mistake, be resilient. Don't chase after it. Don't try to defend it. Don't throw good money after it. Just refocus the team on another solution that serves the mission and move on.

John Foster Dulles, secretary of state in the Eisenhower administration, observed, "The measure of success is not whether you have a tough problem to deal with, but whether it is the same problem you had last year." A problem solved is a springboard to future success, to bigger and better things. The key is to focus on what you are learning, not on what you are losing. And to develop ever greater resilience. If you do that, then you will open the door to future possibilities.

CHAPTER 11

ENCOURAGE YOUR TEAM TO WELCOME RISK

Perhaps the ultimate indicator of resilience is the willingness to take risks. By definition, risk implies uncertainty and the possibility of failure. While it's true some people believe they can't or won't fail—usually because they are too young to understand the risk or too arrogant to believe it applies to them—most reasonable people acknowledge the possibility that their effort could fall short. That implies they believe they can bounce back. That's resilience.

LIFE IS RISK

The reality is that *everything* in life carries some level of risk. If you wanted to avoid all risk, then . . .

- You shouldn't ride in an automobile—they cause 20 percent of all fatal accidents.
- Never travel by air, rail, or water—16 percent of all accidents result from these activities.
- Avoid walking in the street—15 percent of all accidents occur there.
- And definitely don't stay at home—17 percent of all accidents happen there.[1]

In life, there really are no safe places or risk-free activities. Helen Keller, author, speaker, and advocate for the disabled, asserted, "Security is mostly a superstition. It does not exist in nature, nor do the children of men as a whole experience it. Avoiding danger is no safer in the long run than outright exposure. Life is either a daring adventure or nothing." Wouldn't you rather life a daring adventure? Don't you also desire that for your team?

It's true that you and your team risk failure if you try something bold, because you might miss it. But you will also risk failure if you stand still and don't try anything new. As G. K. Chesterton said, "I do not believe in a fate that falls on men however they act; but I do believe in a fate that falls on them unless they act." The less you venture out, the greater your risk of failure. Ironically, the more you risk failure—and actually fail—the greater your chances of success. If you can embrace that idea and convince your team members to do the same, you position yourselves to achieve more.

THE LESS YOU VENTURE OUT, THE GREATER YOUR RISK OF FAILURE.

When it comes to taking risks, I believe there are two kinds of people: those who don't dare try new things, and those who don't dare miss them. Take a look at the differences between the two:

DON'T-DARE-TRY-IT PEOPLE	DON'T-DARE-MISS-IT PEOPLE
They *resist* opportunities.	They *find* opportunities.
They *rationalize* their responsibilities.	They *finish* their responsibilities.
They *rehearse* impossibilities.	They *feed* on impossibilities.
They *rain* on enthusiasm.	They *fan the flame* of enthusiasm.
They *review* their inadequacies.	They *face* their inadequacies.
They *recoil* at the failure of others.	They *figure out* why others fail.
They *reject* the personal cost involved.	They *finance* the cost into their lifestyle.
They *replace* goals with pleasure.	They *find* pleasure in the goal.
They *rejoice* that they have not failed.	They *fear* futility, not failure.
They *rest* before they finish.	They *finish* before they rest.
They *resist* leadership.	They *follow* leaders.
They *remain* unchanged.	They *force* change.

They *replay* the problems.	They *fish* for solutions.
They *rethink* their commitment.	They *fulfill* their commitments.
They *reverse* their decision.	They *finalize* their decision.

The motto of don't-dare-try-it people is: I would rather try nothing great and succeed than try something great and risk failure. The motto of don't-dare-miss-it people is: I would rather try something great and fail than try nothing great and succeed. If you want to accomplish much, you must take chances. That is the only way to increase your odds of success. As Henry C. Link expressed it, "While one person hesitates because he feels inferior, the other is busy making mistakes and becoming superior."

TRAPS THAT MAKE PEOPLE BACK AWAY FROM RISK

If risk has such great potential rewards, then why aren't more people embracing it? I believe they shrink back from risk because they tend to fall into one or more of the following six traps:

> "WHILE ONE PERSON HESITATES BECAUSE HE FEELS INFERIOR, THE OTHER IS BUSY MAKING MISTAKES AND BECOMING SUPERIOR."—HENRY C. LINK

1. THE EMBARRASSMENT TRAP

Deep down, nobody wants to look bad. And if you take a risk and fall flat on your face, you might embarrass yourself. So what. We need to get over that. The only way to become better is to take steps forward—even shaky ones that cause you to fall down. Little progress is better than no progress at all. Success comes in taking many small steps. If you stumble in a small step, it rarely matters. Don't gift wrap the garbage. Let little failures go, and convince your team to see failure the same way.

2. THE RATIONALIZATION TRAP

People who get caught in the rationalization trap second-guess everything they do, and as they prepare to take action, they say to themselves, "Maybe it's really not that important." But the truth is, if you wait long enough, *nothing* is important. Or as a certain rule of procrastination states: "Spend sufficient time confirming the need, and the need will disappear." Don't allow people on your team to think that way.

Sydney J. Harris says, "Regret for the things we did can be tempered by time; it is regret for the things we did not do that is inconsolable." If you and your team take risks and fail, you'll have fewer regrets than if you do nothing and fail.

"REGRET FOR THE THINGS WE DID CAN BE TEMPERED BY TIME; IT IS REGRET FOR THE THINGS WE DID NOT DO THAT IS INCONSOLABLE."—SYDNEY J. HARRIS

---

3. THE UNREALISTIC EXPECTATION TRAP

For some reason, many people think everything in life should be easy, and when they find out that achievement takes effort, they give up. But success takes hard work. Encourage it.

There's a Latin proverb that says, "If there is no wind, row." As you and your team prepare to take a risk, don't expect to get a favorable wind. Begin with the mindset that you will have to row. Then if you get some help from the wind, it will be a pleasant surprise.

"IF THERE IS NO WIND, ROW."—LATIN PROVERB

4. THE FAIRNESS TRAP

Psychologist M. Scott Peck begins his book *The Road Less Traveled* with the words: "Life is difficult." That's true for everyone, but it's *much* harder for some than it is for others. That's not fair, is it? But we need to learn to accept it just the same. Remind your team that part of being resilient is acknowledging life's difficulties and moving on instead of expending energy trying to find fairness. Otherwise, instead of adapting, they are likely to say to themselves, "I shouldn't have to be the one to do this."

Dick Butler said, "Life isn't fair. It isn't going to be fair. Stop sniveling and whining and go out and make it happen for you." Wishing that a risk wasn't yours to take won't make it any easier. In fact, it might make it harder. Everyone's attitude is a choice. Ask your team members to choose to be positive in the face of risk.

5. THE TIMING TRAP

Don Marquis, the famous writer and humorist, was known to be a terrible procrastinator. A friend who knew of this tendency asked him how he ever got his day's work done. "That's simple," said Marquis. "I just pretend that it's yesterday's."

Some people think there will be a perfect time to do everything—and now isn't that time. So they wait. But Jim Stovall advises, "Don't wait for all the lights to be green before you leave the house." If you and your team wait for perfect timing, you'll wait forever. And the more you wait, the more tired you'll get. As William James said, "There is nothing so fatiguing as the eternal hanging on of an uncompleted task." Don't use timing as an excuse. Don't procrastinate. Take action.

"LIFE ISN'T FAIR. IT ISN'T GOING TO BE FAIR. STOP SNIVELING AND WHINING AND GO OUT AND MAKE IT HAPPEN FOR YOU."—DICK BUTLER

6. THE INSPIRATION TRAP

Someone once said, "You don't have to be great to start, but you have to start to be great." Many people want to wait for inspiration before they are willing to step out and take a risk. I find that's especially true of people with an artistic bent. But as playwright Oscar Wilde said, when he was asked the difference between a professional writer and an amateur, the difference is that an amateur writes when he feels like it; a professional writes regardless.

"THERE IS NOTHING SO FATIGUING AS THE ETERNAL HANGING ON OF AN UNCOMPLETED TASK."—WILLIAM JAMES

When it comes to moving forward, Bill Glass gives this advice: "When you get an insight or inspiration, do something about it in twenty-four hours—or the odds are against your ever acting on it."

ARE YOU TAKING ENOUGH RISKS?

As you lead your team, consider whether you are taking enough risks—not senseless ones but intelligent ones.

Even if you or your team members don't fall into one of the six traps, you still may be playing it too safe. How can you tell? By looking at the number and frequency of your mistakes.

Noted Pittsburgh businessman and civic leader Fletcher L. Byrom said this:

> Make sure you generate a reasonable number of mistakes. I know that comes naturally to some people, but too many executives are so afraid of error that they rigidify their organization with checks and counterchecks, discourage innovation, and, in the end, so structure themselves that they will miss the kind of offbeat opportunity that can send a company skyrocketing. So take a look at your record, and if you can come to the end of a year and see that you haven't made any mistakes, then I say, brother, you just haven't tried everything you should have tried.

If your team is succeeding in everything it does, then you and your team are probably not pushing hard enough. And that means you're not taking enough risks.

The willingness to take greater risks is a major key to

achieving success, and you may be surprised that it can solve two very different kinds of problems. First, if you've been hitting all the goals you set for yourself, then you need to increase your willingness to take chances. The road to the next level is always uphill, so you can't coast there.

Conversely, if you find yourself in a place where it seems as if you don't achieve many of your goals, you may be playing it too safe. Once again, the answer is a willingness to take greater risks. It's ironic that opposite ends of the spectrum come together in the area of risk.

What's the solution? Give your team members a failure quotient. Tell them you expect them to fail a certain percentage of the time, then hold them to it. In team meetings, ask them to report not just on their successes but also on how they failed and why. At first, some people will be reluctant to admit their mistakes or failures. Don't let them get away with it. Challenge them. Push them to risk more. Eventually, people will become more open and honest about what isn't working. Congratulate them on their misses.

You will begin to see a shift in the amount of risk

people take. When that happens, you can start discussing which risks were smart and which were foolish. You can teach them to weigh the costs of misses versus safe successes. And you will begin to learn the risk tolerance of your team members. You will also be able to gauge their resilience by their reaction to risk and failure. All this will help the team to achieve more. And when trouble outside of your control comes, your team will be in a better place to weather the storm, bounce back, and move forward stronger than before.

CONCLUSION

If you followed all the advice I've given in this book, you will become more resilient. You will be able to handle adversity with greater confidence. You will no longer be afraid of trouble. You'll see problems as solvable, failure as normal, and setbacks as temporary. When bad luck and misfortune find you, you may go down, but you will bounce back. You will become a much better leader because of your flexibility, adaptability, and resourcefulness.

With those qualities under your belt, if you train your team to handle adversity, overcome their fears, embrace change, welcome risk, and solve problems, they will not only become more resilient as individuals, but they will also form and function as a highly resilient team.

When that happens, together you will be able weather

any storm. Overcome any obstacle. Handle any adverse conditions. You will be nearly unbeatable, not because you won't fail, but because nothing can stop you. You will always bounce back. And when that's true, you always have a chance to win.

NOTES

CHAPTER 1

1. *Resiliency Rules Report: New Research Reveals How to Survive and Thrive Amidst Disruption*, SAS, 2023, https://www.sas.com/content/dam/SAS/documents/corporate-collateral/brochures/en-resiliency-rules-113364.pdf, 5.
2. Adapted from Dr. Chérie Carter-Scott's "Rules for Being Human," accessed September 4, 2025, https://www.drcherie.com/media/rules-for-being-human-2/.
3. Elizabeth M. Fowler, "Careers; After A Business Fails," *New York Times*, May 30, 1984, https://www.nytimes.com/1984/05/30/business/careers-after-a-business-fails.html.
4. Often attributed to business management author Tom Peters.
5. Robert M. McMath and Thom Forbes, *What Were They Thinking?* (Random House, 1998).
6. Kyle Yu and Joel Litman, "Sergio Zyman's 'New Coke': How Can You Take the Biggest Blunder and Turn It into a Cash

Cow? Monday Marketing Marvels," January 22, 2020, https://www.valens-research.com/dynamic-marketing-communique/sergio-zymans-new-coke-how-can-you-take-the-biggest-blunder-and-turn-it-into-a-cash-cow-monday-marketing-marvels/.

7. Philippians 4:11 NKJV.
8. Sometimes attributed to Thomas Edison.

CHAPTER 2

1. Gary Hamel and C. K. Prahalad, *Competing for the Future* (Harvard Business School Press, 1994), 51–52.
2. Author and source unknown.
3. James Chen, "Barings Bank Collapse: A Case Study in Oversight and Banking Crises," Investopedia, updated August 30, 2025, https://www.investopedia.com/terms/b/baringsbank.asp.
4. This sentence paraphrases a statement that has been attributed to General Peyton C. March.

CHAPTER 3

1. Helen Hayes, *On Reflection: An Autobiography* (Fawcett Crest, 1969), 155.
2. This observation, worded somewhat differently, is also made by Paul Pearsall in his book *The Last Self-Help Book You'll Ever Need*.
3. Christopher Logue, "Come to the Edge," 2003; as presented at https://www.poemhunter.com/poem/come-to-the-edge/.

4. Attributed to "R. H. Headlee," exact source unknown.
5. Warren Bennis, *Leaders on Leadership* (Harvard Business School Press, 1992).
6. Harold C. Warlick Jr., *Conquering Loneliness* (Word Books, 1979).

CHAPTER 4

1. Arthur Freeman and Rose DeWolf, *The 10 Dumbest Mistakes Smart People Make and How to Avoid Them: Simple and Sure Techniques for Gaining Greater Control of Your Life* (HarperCollins, 1992).
2. Patricia Sellers, "Now Bounce Back," *Fortune*, May 1, 1995, p. 49.
3. *Annual Report 2024*, Home Depot, accessed April 26, 2025, https://ir.homedepot.com/~/media/Files/H/HomeDepot-IR/2025/HD_2024_AR_IRsite_v2.pdf.

CHAPTER 5

1. Denis Waitley, *The Winner's Edge* (Berkley, 1986).
2. Ernest H. Rosenbaum and Isadora R. Rosenbaum, "Attitude—The Will to Live," Cancer Supportive Care Programs National and International, reprinted from Coping with Cancer, March/April 1999, http://www.cancersupportivecare.com/attitude.html#Mind, accessed September 23, 2005.
3. Rosenbaum and Rosenbaum, "Attitude—The Will to Live."
4. John Milton, *Paradise Lost*, Book I, line 253.

CHAPTER 6

1. Becky Brodin, "The Key to Bouncing Back," *Discipleship Journal* 109 (1999): 67.
2. "Where Failures Get Fixed," *Fortune*, May 1, 1995, p. 64.

CHAPTER 7

1. Don Shula and Ken Blanchard, *Everyone's a Coach* (Harper Business, 1995), 177.
2. Jim Zabloski, *The 25 Most Common Problems in Business* (Broadman and Holman, 1996), 88.

CHAPTER 8

1. Dennis Waitley, *Seeds of Greatness* (Pocket, 1988).
2. As presented at https://reemusboxing.com/cus-damato-quotes/.
3. Barbara Bush, address to Kennebunk (Maine) High School, source unknown.
4. Author unknown.

CHAPTER 9

1. David Bayles and Ted Orland, *Art and Fear* (Capra Press, 1993), 57.
2. Frances Hodgson Burnett, *The Secret Garden* (Harper Trophy, 1998), 337.

CHAPTER 10

1. As quoted in the October 16, 1920 issue of *Forbes* magazine, in an interview conducted by Bertie Charles Forbes, and titled "How to Communicate with the New World."
2. Tom Zuercher, "And Let It Begin with Me," http://www.brethren.org/AC2001/Zuercher.htm.
3. Richard Reeves, *President Reagan: The Triumph of Imagination* (Simon and Schuster, 2005).

CHAPTER 11

1. *The Joyful Noiseletter.*

ABOUT THE AUTHOR

John C. Maxwell is a #1 *New York Times* bestselling author, speaker, coach, and leader who has sold more than 36 million books in fifty languages. He is the founder of Maxwell Leadership®—the leadership development organization created to expand the reach of his principles of helping people lead powerful, positive change. Maxwell's books and programs have been translated into 70 languages and have been used to train tens of millions of leaders in every nation. His work also includes that of the Maxwell Leadership Foundation and EQUIP, nonprofit organizations that have impacted millions of adults and youth across the globe through values-based, people-centric leadership training.

John has been recognized as the #1 leader i
ness by the American Management Association and as the world's most influential leadership expert by both *Business Insider* and *Inc.* magazine. He is a recipient of the Horatio Alger Award and the Mother Teresa Prize for Global Peace and Leadership from the Luminary Leadership Network.

Maxwell and the work of Maxwell Leadership continue to influence individuals and organizations worldwide—from *Fortune* 500 CEOs and national leaders to entrepreneurs and the leaders of tomorrow. For more information about him and Maxwell Leadership, visit MaxwellLeadership.com.

LEADERSHIFT

In *Leadershift: The 11 Essential Changes Every Leader Must Embrace,* leadership expert and bestselling author John C. Maxwell teaches how to accelerate your career by putting your leadership into high gear. Providing a blueprint for change, he shares the shifts he made during his long and successful career. Among those leadershifts are

- The Improvement Shift—from Team Uniformity to Team Diversity
- The Abundance Shift—from Maintaining to Creating
- The Reproduction Shift—from Ladder Climbing to Ladder Building
- The Impact Shift—from Trained Leaders to Transformational Leaders

Gain insight and guidance so that you can embrace these shifts and put them into action. Then stay ahead of the curve by not only relying on speed but thriving on timing, innovating, and making changes before they are necessary.

Instead of staying the course, you can change your trajectory and position yourself for new and exciting achievements.